FI[illegible] THE HOLE

Dalen Garris

FIRE IN THE HOLE

Dalen Garris

Pleasant Word
A Division of WINEPRESS PUBLISHING

Pleasant Word (a division of WinePress Publishing, PO Box 428, Enumclaw, WA 98022) functions only as book publisher. As such, the ultimate design, content, editorial accuracy, and views expressed or implied in this work are those of the author.

All Scripture references are taken from the King James Version of the Bible.

ISBN 1-4141-0376-X
Library of Congress Catalog Card Number: 2005900554

Table of Contents

Introduction

I HAVE BEEN ASKED MANY TIMES WHERE THE NAME *FIRE IN THE HOLE* CAME from and what does it signify. It's a funny story. Minutes before my very first radio broadcast, the DJ asked me the name of my program. I was caught completely off guard. I hadn't thought about a name and had but seconds to come up with an answer. I shot up a quick prayer, and an immediate answer came down. "Fire in the Hole" I quipped, not knowing what it stood for nor where I had heard that expression before. Being as puzzled as anyone, I did some research.

"Fire in the hole" is an old miner's term that is also used in the military. It is shouted out whenever an explosion is about to go off. You don't have to reach very far to grasp the analogy that the Lord gave me. There's an explosion of spiritual war that is about to occur, just as the Word of God states. The question is not whether or not it will take place, but will we be ready for it when it does.

The articles that make up this book were written as a series of newspaper columns in anticipation of that explosion. At the time, there didn't seem to be much connection between one column and another—I would write as the Lord impressed me to—but over the long run I began to perceive the weaving of a tapestry in these messages that could only be seen in its overall design from a distance.

The message brought forth in this book is an old message, but still relevant today. I agree with Solomon that the more things change, the more they stay the same. I can only hope that you will see the tapestry here as the integrated workmanship of the Master of design, who has not given up on us, but ever calls us back to Him.

CHAPTER ONE

Spiritual Warfare

Conflict

Warfare is something we don't mind reading about, but we are often uncomfortable thinking about it in our own lives. Conflict is, however, one of the central themes of Christianity. God is always looking for someone through whom he may declare war on the enemy. He doesn't raise up prayer socializers; He raises up prayer warriors. The great men of God that we see throughout the Bible were warriors who marched into fierce conflict proclaiming victory, armed with nothing but a vision for God, faith in His power, and the Word of God as their sword.

We often think that warfare is good for someone else, but not for us. But is it really up to others to storm the gates of Hell, while we sit back, comfortable with the thought that because we go to church every Sunday we're OK? Let someone else fight. We just want to relax and be raptured. Oh, we'll send them money, but will we actively engage the enemy?

After the invasion of Omaha Beach on D-Day, it was determined that one reason the battle was so bloody was that only one out of five soldiers had actually been able to fire their weapons. Firepower has got to be brought to bear if we expect to win whether it is a physical or spiritual battle. Are you firing the weapons that God has given you at the enemy? Are you fighting as if your life depended on it?

When we buy into the ecumenical doctrines of compromise, we lower our weapons. When we allow the enemy to infiltrate our communities, our schools, our TV, and every other aspect of our society, we step down from the warrior's stand that we have been called to. Is it more important to be nice than to stand up and fight for the righteousness of God?

Have we have been so saturated with the "Love" gospel for the last thirty or so years that our churches are afraid of offending someone and, as a result, have loosened their grip on their weapons and will no longer fight? Why has our attitude changed? And what are the consequences?

What was once the dominion of God's people is now enemy territory. Satan will not give back this territory without a fight. He will attack anyone who dares make a stand against him, and few are willing to war against him. There is a price to pay that is much higher than what it takes to get up and go to church on Sunday. But either we will put on the armor of God and fight, or we will go down in defeat. There is no comfortable middle ground.

An "easy" Gospel is just that—easy. But there's no easy way out of this battle. Either we will stand for the honor of God, or we will ultimately succumb to the "...**hour of temptation, which shall come upon all the world, to try them that dwell upon the earth**" Revelation 3:10.

A Call to Arms

And Jonathan said to the young man that bare his armor, Come, and let us go over unto the garrison of these uncircumcised: it may be that the Lord will work for us: for there is no restraint to the Lord to save by many or by few.

1 Samuel 14:6

In this passage, we see the people of God hiding in rocks and dens from what seemed to be an overwhelming situation. The enemy had amassed thousands of warriors to destroy the people of God, but there were a couple of men who not only believed God, but also were willing to take the battle to the enemy and trust God for the outcome. It took more than espousing a good religion; it took a spirit of war in their souls and a fire in their hearts to fight for the honor of God.

We stand here in these last days in a similar situation. We see the Church relegated to a position of maintaining the status quo, but it is not on-fire enough to stand up and fight. We have heard of great moves of God in the past, but are we willing to stand in the gap and clamor up the rocks to battle for a revival in our churches? Are we willing to pay the price, no matter the cost? If not, then we are dying on the Vine.

The Lord is a mighty man of war, and we need strong men of God invested with His power, strength, and authority to lead the charge. We don't need nice preachers, delivering nice messages to nice people so we can have a lot of nice churches. The Word of God is full of warnings of the encroaching power of darkness to take over this world and destroy the Church. Where are the Jonathan's, the David's, the fiery prophets, the real strong men and women of God that we have read about who are willing to resist unto blood?

To bring about a really powerful move of God that will send the enemy running, it takes a people who are willing to fight for the honor of God, who will storm the gates of hell, and petition the throne of God and not retreat. The battle may be the Lord's, but He requires some mighty men and women of God to take up the battle. He will not send a revival to a people who don't care enough to stand up and fight for one. There is a call to arms, but how many are ready to answer the call?

The move of God we need starts with prayer. That's where the battle is won or lost. And not just a simple prayer or two, but desperate, strong, prevailing prayer that is dedicated to holding up the Blood-Stained Banner and claiming the victory that is so desperately needed in these last days. Remember, it's not the hearers that are just before God. It's the doers.

Somebody has to get on their knees.

The Death of Saul

... and the men of Israel fled from before the Philistines and fell down slain in mount Gilboa.

(1 Samuel 31:1)

Where did Saul go wrong? He was handpicked by Almighty God to lead His people Israel. And yet, in his fall we see the triumph of the powers of darkness over the people of God.

Had God forsaken His people? Or had his people forsaken Him?

Saul began his reign as king with God's hand on him, but quickly assumed a superior attitude of authority over the people of Israel based on how he perceived his position. Thinking that he had kept the commandment of the Lord (1 Samuel 15:31), he soon began to rely on his own authority and forsook the Almighty God who had anointed him in the first place.

When Saul finally died, the Philistines made the most of it. What rejoicing there was in halls of darkness! They displayed his head all over the country and nailed his body to the wall of Bethshan for display. They sang and danced in their streets as they smacked their curled lips over the spoils of war.

Reliance on pride and established authority is in direct conflict with the authority of God. Saul was a type of carnal religion—an analogy of an established church in preeminence over the people of God. Those who walk in carnal religiosity may strive to assume the robes of spiritual authority, but they always lack the source of real power. Appearances are often deceptive and can fool those who sincerely want to walk with God, but in the end only those like David, whose source of power comes from the Throne of God, will prevail. God will always raise up a David.

If we are to emerge victorious over the encroaching darkness that we see overtaking America, we cannot rely on our membership in a religion. "Church as usual" has no power over sin, neither is it a bulwark against the pressing waves of darkness that constantly crash against the moral foundations of our society. We need to be like David and take the battle to the Lord and walk in the depths of His power. Only when we are armed with the power of God can we ever attempt to fight the enemy. You cannot fight spiritual battles with carnal weapons.

The Philistines saw the death of Saul as a victory. I see it as the opening of a great door through which David led the people back to God, clothed in His anointed power.

Détente

Détente is a word we associate with the Cold War. It conjures up pictures of the Evil Empire, the SALT arms reductions, peaceful cohabitation, a reduction of nuclear fears, successful negotiations, and overall relief. It's a French word that means, "slackened bowstrings." I suppose that détente can seem like a good alternative when you're faced with worldwide annihilation.

In warfare, however, there are four positions that can be taken—offense, defense, détente, and desertion. Ask any general, and he'll tell you the only position worth taking is the offense. Take up the defense, and you'll end up losing. Succumb to détente, and you'll be back at war again, but this time you'll be at a decided disadvantage. Desert and you deserve to be shot.

When we consider life from the spiritual perspective, we have to be aware that we are in the fiercest of all wars. The spoils are not political or philosophical gain, but the eternal souls of mankind. There is no discharge in this war until the end of time. Our enemy is cunning and sly, vicious and cold-blooded, patient and unrelenting. The only compromise that he will make with us is one that will end up in his favor.

And yet, just like in real war, we grow tired of the struggle that spiritual warfare brings. After Joshua entered Canaan, the next generation was more interested in going back to a "normal" life and worked out a détente with the peoples of the land. Their decision led to their downfall years later.

If we slacken our bowstrings and allow ourselves to go back to a "normal" lifestyle, we will shortly end up on the defense, fighting a desperate uphill battle for our own survival. That's how secular humanism entered our schools, as well as evolution, abortion, and forced acceptance of homosexuality. We relaxed and loosened our armor. We accepted a more easy-going, socially acceptable Gospel, a smoother set of Bible translations, and an easier set of rules to live our lives by. It's human nature to want to relax, but the price of commitment to the cause of Christ is too high only when we are satisfied with something less than total victory.

Paul never relaxed. His warnings were aimed at strengthening us for warfare, dressed in battle armor and standing strong. He didn't "smile a good smile." He "fought a good fight." He didn't compromise with heresy for the sake of religious unity. He knew the devil's wiles and gave no place to him at all. If you let down your guard, Satan will eat your lunch, then pop your bag.

You know what I'd like to see more than anything else? I'd like to see the old-fashioned warriors of God stand up and raise the bloodstained banner with the war cry of those who will never give in, never give up, and never accept compromise. To do anything less in this last hour would be to let down the saints that have gone on before us who have handed us the baton in this relay race. This is the last stretch in this great battle for men's souls. Now is the time to carry on the battle to the finish line and claim the victory that is ours. To quote a popular song, "If you don't stand for something, you'll fall for anything."

Conspiracy

There are more views of world history than the average guy can keep up with. It seems like everyone has a different perspective on what drives the forces of human events. Alongside traditional historical viewpoints, there is the Conspiratorial Theory of world history. In essence, this viewpoint states there is a long-running plan devised by an elite and powerful group to bring the entire world into the unified submission of a feudal type of society. This fascinating topic has been the subject of numerous books, political groups, talk-show radio, and uncounted grass-roots organizations. Unfortunately, there is a certain amount of disagreement on the particulars of how, why, and when the world will succumb to this New World Order. After a while, you hear so many different takes on the subject that the average American doesn't know what to believe, or whether to believe anything at all.

Wouldn't it be nice if you could just roll over and all this stuff would just go away? Let everybody else get all excited. Please, just let me go to work, raise my family, go to church on Sunday, and live a normal decent life. What's wrong with that? Does everybody have to march down Main St. waving the flag and shouting slogans?

But what if the New World Order is true? Or any of the other conspiratorial theories? Just what is the average guy supposed to do? Do we jump into political action groups? Or, do we start the 2nd American Revolution? Are we really going to lose all our freedoms?

Or is that just a bunch of babble from some frustrated armchair warriors who read Tom Clancy books?

Have I struck a chord with most of you out there?

About now, you're probably wondering which side I'm on. Let me give you a hint. Skip to the verse at the end of the chapter.

Regardless of how you stand on political issues, only the Word of God is sure. The Bible shows that we are most definitely moving into a one-world government and religion, but it also shows the source as being different from the political/financial entities that are usually cited. The Mother of every abomination on earth, and the source of all this wickedness, is spiritual in nature.

You may resist, and you should, but you will never win spiritual warfare with carnal endeavors. What we need is a Holy Ghost Revival to bring people into a walk in the Spirit of the Lord. Only then will we be able to resist and withstand the demonic onslaught that is about to sweep the world.

It's more than just going to church on Sunday, or just living a good life. Our very survival depends on it.

> *Put on the whole armor of God, that ye may be able to stand against the wiles of the devil. For we wrestle not against flesh and blood, but against principalities, against powers, against the rulers of the darkness of this world, against spiritual wickedness in high places. Wherefore take unto you the whole armor of God, that ye may be able to withstand in the evil day, and having done all, to stand*
>
> *Ephesians 6:11-13.*

The Cycle of Apostasy

And an angel of the LORD came up from Gilgal to Bochim, and said, I made you to go up out of Egypt, and have brought you unto the land which I sware unto your fathers; and I said, I will never break my covenant with you.

And ye shall make no league with the inhabitants of this land; ye shall throw down their altars: but ye have not obeyed my voice: why have ye done this?
Judges 2:1,2

The answer to that question is Compromise. Religious compromise is the tendency of human nature to shy away from spiritual warfare.

There is a cycle that repeats itself throughout the Word of God. One generation answers God's call to charge into the battle; the next generation enjoys the fruits of their victory; then the next set of generations relaxes into an apostasy and compromise.

Then God sends prophets to call His people to repentance, but they are persecuted and killed. However, a seed grows out of the ensuing conflict, and another generation will rise up to answer the call to battle again.

Victory does not come through compromise, but through warriors that will make a stand for Truth. These warriors never seem to come from established institutions. Instead, the Lord calls forth his prophets out of nowhere without any recognized credentials. That is true from Moses, through the prophets, to John the Baptist; from Jesus, through the apostles, unto today. He even used a jackass at one point! (Numbers 22:28)

Could it be that it is not the messenger that is important, but rather the message? Is it because the Lord is looking for those who will respond to righteousness and Truth, instead of the personality of some exalted celebrity? Or perhaps our religious institutions are too apostate to produce warriors for God.

I believe we are in the slough of the last one of those cycles of apostasy. Churches are on every corner, but there is a lack of a manifestation of the power of God and hardly any call to battle. Everywhere I turn, I hear of preachers encouraging their people to, "put aside their petty differences" and create, "unity with all the churches, but Ephesians chapter four addresses the unity of the Body of Christ through righteousness and walking in the Spirit of God—not through compromise. There is no compromise with the Devil.

While many are looking with apprehension for bombs, and tanks, and UN troops, the Word of God tells us that the Antichrist will win the kingdom with flatteries. Many will fall for this unified one-world church movement because it sounds so nice. We have fallen so deeply into our apostasy that we can no longer recognize the flattery of Satan, but actually mistake it for the voice of God.

What a dramatic difference from how many of our evangelical denominations were founded. Many of those churches were forged in the fires of revival and their church fathers paid the price of blood and persecution to establish the power of a real Gospel. It has been handed over, however, to a generation who has let the fire go out, has lost the resolve to fight for Truth, and is willing to compromise with the Devil for the sake of peace.

And there is a stirring in the graveyard as our church fathers roll over in their graves.

Compromise in Battle

A town was on the news not long ago that was about to defy the Supreme Court ruling against prayer at High School football games. I was excited to hear that they were going to stand up for what they believed in, but at the last moment, they backed down and said they would humbly comply.

It reminded me of the passage in the Bible that relates how David and two of his mighty men stood in a barley field against the entire Philistine army, right after all Israel had fled They were not mindless robots that had no comprehension of the situation they were facing. I'm sure they felt the acrid taste of fear on the back of their tongue, and I doubt they spoke a word to each other as they gripped their weapons in anticipation of the battle and watched as thousands of warriors descended upon them. They faced an almost sure death with a courage that was born out of an honor that had its foundation in faith.

These were not men that faced death thinking that everything was just going to turn out just fine because God loved them. They decided to make a stand for God no matter what happened. They would not run; they would not surrender; and they refused to compromise. They would fight for the honor of God. What would these men have done if they were here at a High School football game?

Today, it seems as if "compromise" is the buzzword of this generation. Compromise might be admirable in politics and business, but in ministry it reeks with the scent of sin, weakness and death. In ministry, you are supposed to stand up and fight for what is right and not give in to the powers of darkness. A genuine fear of God is needed to give you the strength to do this. Compromise usually comes when you don't have the fire inside you to stand up against what everybody else thinks is OK.

We hear from ministers who say they would rather run away from a fight than stand in battle—all in the interest of peace and unity. What are they afraid of? And with whom are they trying to have peace and unity? The Devil? Is this what we want to teach our children?

I blame the so-called Bible colleges and seminaries. In their pursuit of a carnal knowledge of God, they have created ministers of the Gospel that have had the fire sucked right out of them. We don't have the real men of God that we once had; we have nice guys that wouldn't harm a flea. Give me those old-fashioned preachers that once thundered from the pulpits with the uncompromised Word of God. Compromise only brings "church as usual." No guts, no glory; no battle, no victory.

As a result, a generation has been fostered that accepts homosexuality as an "alternative," but condemns prayer in school. It's OK to kill babies, but not trees. Murderers are set free, while the rights to self-defense are whittled away. Sex, violence, foul language, and immorality are OK on TV because it's only TV and it isn't real. Premarital sex is OK, because everyone is doing it.

Find some warriors that are willing to stand in that field of barley and fight for what is right—win, lose, or draw—and I'll show you the seeds for a revival in this land that are long overdue.

Wise in Your Own Eyes

Be not wise in thine own eyes: fear the LORD, and depart from evil.

Proverbs 3:7

Over the years, I have seen one ministry after another that had been founded on a strong Gospel fall into irrelevancy. Many of them promised to be great moves of God, but ended up being not much more than large organizations that only fed themselves. No longer driven by the Spirit of the Lord, they pressed forward under their own desire to build bigger and better organizations, but they no longer had that deep, vibrant power that resonates with a real leading from the Holy Ghost.

I believe in the supernatural outpourings of God because I've been there when the Spirit of the Lord would fall down so hard that you didn't even know if you were still on the face of the Earth. Hoopin', hollerin', and doing rain dances in the flesh, however, will no more call down the fire of God than it did for the priests of Baal at Elijah's sacrifice.

What happened to these ministries? They do not reflect the strong men of God of the past like John Wesley, William Booth, Charles Moody, Billy Sunday, and many others of whom we still hear the thundering echoes of the Word of God. Although many of today's mega-minstiries have become household names, they have not retained that same power in God that they had when they started.

The pattern of recurring factors we see in the great carnal endeavors of these huge ministries is a desire for power and a lack of the fear of God. A very subtle change oftentimes slips into a ministry as it begins to grow. Leaders who are not humbled by the awesome fear of God begin to become wise in their own eyes, and become enamored with their own abilities, their own wisdom, and their own supposed place in God. Human nature is such that, given the opportunity, it will choose to think well of itself. True subjection to the Spirit of God, however, does not lie along that comfortable path which is so easy to fall into.

Freedom in the Spirit does not mean freedom to allow your own spirit to take charge. True humility in a man of God can only be maintained by a complete denial of self and a total crucified walk that is in subjection to the Spirit of God. When we allow ourselves to be seduced by our own spirit, our ways, and the way we think things should be, we chase away the Spirit of God, and the light from our church's candlestick becomes dimmer and dimmer until it no longer shines with the glory of God.

Isaiah 29, states that the fear of God cannot be taught by the precept of men, but comes through standing before the awesome presence of the Almighty, holy, living God who dwells in righteousness, and knowing that we are but dust and ashes. When we stand before Him in such a way, we receive holy boldness, strong confidence, and a wisdom that our flesh will never be able to comprehend nor duplicate. It is the fear of God that keeps us in the way of righteousness and allows the Lord to have His way in our lives and in our ministries. When we forget that, we forget that our power comes from God, and we fall prey to our own desires for power and recognition. It will destroy a ministry every time.

Only when we allow ourselves to be led by the Spirit of God will we be able to bear forth fruit that will last into eternity.

The Making of Champions

There is ample evidence that God supernaturally intervened in behalf of the colonists in order for them to resist the British, never mind actually win the Revolutionary War. The deck wasn't just stacked against them—they didn't hold any cards! Except one. Time and time again, the hand of God could be seen as the rag-tag group of farmers marched toward victory over the largest and strongest army and navy in the entire world.

Somebody forgot to tell them that it was a useless cause. Somebody forgot to tell them that they couldn't win, that it was a waste of human lives to try, that values didn't really matter, and that some causes just aren't worth dying for. Somebody forgot to tell them all the things that make for common sense. But even if they did know all if this, it wouldn't have mattered, because they believed that their cause was right before God.

At that time, America was still hot from the fires of revival that had just swept the land in a move called the Great Awakening. These were born-again Christians who not only took God at His Word, but also were willing to hold up the precepts and values of Truth above all other things. They were sorely tested and tried, but we are free today because of these men and women of God who refused to compromise their integrity.

I believe that persecution will once again descend upon the real on-fire Christians—those who will not surrender their strong stand for the Gospel (the *real* Gospel, not the one that has been mollified in our churches today to a socially correct "peace & love" message). The Bible tells us twice that the times coming will be worse than have ever been since the beginning of time. The devastation will be strong, but I believe that, once again, there will be men and women who will not care how the odds are stacked against them, what the rest of the society believes, or what price has to be paid for their stand in the Gospel.

Standing on the edge of defeat at the point of utter desperation is where the souls of champions are forged. Where does your power in God come from? Down in the depths of the Valley! Where do you get the grit and determination to drive on? From the sand on that desert floor where you are on your knees crying out before God! Where do you get your depth in God? From the depth of a crucified walk!

Christians who are not willing to pay this price are left with a shallow, insipid Christian walk. They never see the nuggets and jewels of the deep things of God, because these are only found on the bottom of the Valley. They never truly understand the sufferings of the Cross because they have never experienced the heart-swelling poignancy of a life sacrificed to God. Their hearts are not cut deeply over lost souls, because they cannot seem to grasp the wickedness of sin, nor the beauty of holiness.

We need another outpouring of the Spirit of God before the darkness of the Antichrist descends, but the complacent, satisfied structures of religion make poor tinder for the fires of revival. Revival will not come through religion or "church as usual." It comes from a heart-felt realization of our deep need and reliance upon God, Holy Ghost conviction and repentance for our lukewarm apostasy, and a subsequent crying out to God for mercy.

No Small Stir

We read in Colossians that the Laodiceans and Colossians were to read each other's epistles from Paul. What a privilege for these people to receive a letter from Paul! You can almost feel the anticipation in the air. The church at Colossians was under heavy persecution while trying to accomplish the enormous task before them. The whole known world was lying in pagan idolatry and on their way to Hell, but the Christians knew they had the Truth and they were excited!

Jesus was thought of as some new god who had come out of Judea. By itself, that would not have created much of a stir, but Jesus' followers wouldn't let well enough alone. They had to keep preaching their doctrine of salvation, repentance from sin, adherence to commandments (that most flesh did not enjoy), and the constant reproof that anybody who didn't go along with their ideas was going to a place of torment for eternity.

Now the idea of Hades was not new. Different shades of the concept have filtered down through the ages ever since Noah. However, the idea that someone could possibly go there was often mollified by some simple deeds done in the temple. Candles could be lit, incense burnt, or repetitious chants over a string of beads could be muttered. Of course, there would always be a priest there who could intercede before the gods in case these didn't work. Especially to some mother figure like Astarte, who would have compassion because she was a mother and would go talk to God for you. Wasn't that nice of her? Then of course, there were always the statues all around of various gods which all had their own fields of specialty—travel, war, family, love, etc. As long as one showed up at the Temple, you were OK. Sound familiar?

Why did the Christians have to be so pushy? Just because everybody didn't believe their gospel, did that mean everybody was going to Hell? After all, everyone believed in God. As long as you didn't harm anyone, what was so bad about that? Why couldn't they just leave everybody alone?

Persecution was rampant against that early church. It would have been so easy for them to adopt a policy of laissez-faire and be satisfied with gathering together, but there was a great commission hanging over them. They had to win the world for Christ. They plunged into the challenge because they knew, without a doubt, that they had the Truth, and that if they didn't evangelize the world, multitudes of people would be lost forever. God's people have always grown under persecution, but languished in times of peace and prosperity.

Is it so different now? Human nature has never changed. The fashions may change, but the basic nature of man will always exhibit itself in the same ways. There will always be those who are comfortable with a laissez-faire form of religion that makes allowances for the flesh, and would rather not be bothered with something that calls them to a deeper walk in God.

Then there are always those for whom this world is not worthy; those who need nourishment directly from the Throne of God; those who hunger for more than what can be seen with the eyes. They feed on Truth and the life-flowing Spirit of God. Nothing else will do. The great commission hangs over them. There is a whole world out there that is lost and dying, and it's up to us to tell them before it's too late.

What an exciting time to live!

Press Toward the Mark

I press toward the mark for the prize of the high calling of God in Christ Jesus.

Philippians 3:14

It seems that life consists of one struggle after another. No matter what station in life we find ourselves in, there is always one more hill to climb, one more obstacle to overcome, one more battle to fight. Do we ever reach the place where we can finally say that we have arrived? We look at others that have attained a place that appears secure, and think that if we could just get to that point we could relax. Upon a closer look, however, we always find that they also are in an upward struggle for the next level. That's how they reached their present position in the first place. It's a matter of goals.

Religion is often handled differently, however. Most of our denominations were forged in the fires of revival and had to overcome the persecutions that beset their early days. As they became established into the mainstreams of society, their hard, sharp edge became dull.

Time to relax and pull in our horns. We have arrived. Time to pursue after other things in our lives because our religion is now secure. As one old man put it, "We can relax and be raptured" ...as long, of course, as we go to church on Sunday. Oh, we have our little battles, like prayer at the football games, but basically we can assure ourselves that the fierceness of the battle is over. We can get comfortable.

It's like taking a bath. No one likes a cold shower, and we certainly don't want to get scalded with hot water. No, we enjoy that warm, relaxing feeling of a bath with water that is just the right temperature. But God's perspective is a little different. He'd rather you were either hot or cold. His Word says that if you are lukewarm, He will spew you out of His mouth. He wants you to be on fire and to be valiant for the Truth. (Sigh) More battles. Does it ever end?

The fading light that once burned so hotly in our churches is much like the sunset. It comes ever so gradually – even with a mellow glow. All of a sudden, it is night and we have become accustomed to the evening.

Anyone with a bright torch can seem startling, even abrasive. If we remember back to our heritages, however, we see men and women who were warriors and did not know the meaning of compromise. There was no letting up in their pursuit to establish the truth of God in the land. They stood for the honor of God regardless of the cost, and regardless of the odds.

I am reminded of David and his companion in 1 Chronicles 11:13. All Israel had fled before the Philistines, but David and Eleazar stood in that field of barley and refused to run, refused to give in, and refused to compromise, but were willing to fight to the end against overwhelming odds for the honor of God.

Press toward the mark. Run the race to win. Stand for the honor of God, and let your light shine brightly. We are in a war from which there is no discharge until we cross over into Eternity. Be courageous for the truth and fight for the greatest cause of all time.

It is our heritage.

A Field of Barley

He was with David at Pasdammim, and there the Philistines were gathered together to battle, where was a parcel of ground full of barley; and the people fled from before the Philistines. And they set themselves in the midst of that parcel, and delivered it, and slew the Philistines; and the LORD saved them by a great deliverance.

1 Chronicles 11:13,14.

I can hear the wind rustling through the barley field, tugging at David and Eleazar's garments, while they gripped their weapons in quiet determination. I can feel the morning rays of sunshine rising behind them as a silent tension hung in the air. The ominous feeling of battle must have been strong as they set their feet and stood waiting. These were not men who stood because they thought they could beat this army of Philistines, but were men who just would not run. They would not give in; they would not compromise. They would stand to defend the honor of God no matter what, and leave the consequences to Him.

Where are the souls of champions such as these forged? At the very rim of defeat. At the point of desperation. At the place where character and integrity are all that hold you up, and where you have to reach out by faith and take hold of the courage to stand for what you believe regardless of the odds against you. Warriors such as these are not worried about being politically correct, socially correct, or religiously correct. They are made of steel that won't bend—steel that is forged in the fire from the altar before God.

This is the kind of steel needed to form the framework of any church if it is ever to be strong. Weak messages in the pulpit never make strong Christians in the congregation. Nice people and nice churches and nice ministers do not hear the call to battle; neither do they perceive the dark realities of spiritual war. Only those who are hungry and thirsty for the power of God feel the desperate need for revival.

The Lord told the Israelites that their prophets had seen vain and foolish things on their behalf, and had not discovered their iniquity that had led to their captivity. They did not have the guts to tell the people the truth then, and not much has changed since. As long as we are more willing to hear the messages of peace and love, blessings and prosperity rather than the messages of repentance, mercy, and righteousness, we will fall prey to false prophets and allow ourselves to be lulled to sleep, weakened, and ultimately defeated.

Many will allow themselves and their churches to be carried off to a last days ecumenical Babylon. Others will run from the battle, and lose their souls because they just wouldn't take hold of Victory. But there will always be those who will stand in that field of barley and fight for the honor of God.

May God give us all the courage to stand and be valiant for the Truth.

CHAPTER TWO

End Time Warnings

The Coming Rain

By faith Noah, being warned of God of things not seen as yet, moved with fear, prepared an ark to the saving of his house; by which he condemned the world.

Hebrews 11:7

THE LORD IS ALWAYS FAITHFUL TO WARN HIS PEOPLE WHEN JUDGMENT IS ABOUT to fall. There is always time to prepare and find safety. Sometimes that means fleeing for your life, as with Lot; sometimes we get 100 years, as with Noah.

Judgments do not come as a surprise. Throughout history, you can see the pattern hold true. Sin and rebellion in a society always bring an apostasy to the Church at large. Once the Church falls asleep, then judgment begins to fall. Yet God still exhorts us to repent in those final minutes. The false prosperity that usually precedes destruction, however, seems to lull people into a mindset that things will just keep going on as usual and that there's no need to worry or fear.

The warnings that God gives through His prophets and servants is almost always ignored and mocked. Consider how foolish that little-known hairy man named Elijah seemed after he had walked through the lush, green, watered valleys of Israel to tell the king that it wouldn't rain until he said so. Three years later, no one was laughing.

The warnings always come in times of plenty. But once the judgments fall, the time for repentance is over. Noah is a great example of this; once it began to rain, even he couldn't open the door of the ark.

Friend, the time of prosperity is about to come to a close. We will see the fabric of our society and our false prosperity change dramatically for the worse. Judgment is going to fall quickly.

Consider the ways of our nation and society, and tell me if you think we can escape. Great societies of the past suffered terrible judgments and were guilty of far less than we. Is there any nation throughout time that ever escaped after murdering it's own children? Yet we have shed the innocent blood of 45 million babies. And that is only one of the multitudes of sins we are guilty of.

My greatest fear is that the people of God who know the Truth, but who are lulled into an easy-going Gospel, will not hearken to the warnings of God all around them. If they do not move in the fear of the Lord to strengthen themselves in the Word and prayer, then they will not have the strength to stand in that hour of temptation that will come to try the whole world. They need to have the fire and the boldness of the Holy Ghost flowing through them now, not tomorrow.

Don't roll over and go back to sleep. It's about to rain.

The Grasshopper and the Ants

Behold, the hire of the laborers who have reaped down your fields, which is of you kept back by fraud, crieth: and the cries of them which have reaped are entered into the ears of the Lord of sabaoth.

James 5:4

The cold grip of the last days is steadily closing upon us. While many sing and rejoice for the advent of the coming of the Lord, others look to the cold reality of the dark times ahead. The warnings that are in the Word of God are stiff, if we care to search them out, but a more carefree Gospel seems to be the one that is preferred. I look for messages of repentance, Holy Ghost conviction, and of the fear of the Lord, but behold, I see singing and dancing, love and permissiveness, peace and safety. We see what we want, and explain away the rest.

So many of the huge international ministries and denominations have spread themselves out like a giant green bay tree, but they have only produced religions, not revivals. They are very good at consoling us that we are all children of God and have little to worry about, but they shy away from bringing us to the heart-felt conviction that leads to a broken-hearted repentance. They are professionals at fraud, and have held back the end-time harvest. They are clouds without rain, as Peter put it. It is a small wonder there are so many souls that are hungry for something more from God than what they get from church.

If we believe our church bulletins, everything seems to be so wonderful here in our hometown congregations. Everything is just going great! If we believe our Bibles we see spiritual famine and a great falling away, especially in these last days. One perspective is comfortable; one is not. The real question, therefore, is which will we choose to believe?

There is going to be a one-world church soon. Arrangements are already being made, and the church world is pressing into it. It will be a very nice church where everybody will be able to worship together in peace and harmony. There will be no room for harsh, hateful messages, or denominational squabbles. Why, even the Buddhists, Moslems, and Hindus will be part of it. Anyone who really believes in their heart of their own form of God will be welcome. Think I'm kidding? It's already started.

I have been accused at times of being unmerciful, unloving, and heavy-handed. Why buck the flow? Why preach such a "hard" Gospel? Why not take it easy and just preach the love of Jesus? Peace and safety. Prosperity and blessings!

You know what? That sounds just like the story of the Grasshopper and the Ants. Don't worry about winter coming; enjoy the summertime! No matter how we package it, however, messages that are not tempered with the fear of the Lord will only lead us into that comfortable Christian lifestyle so that we can relax and be raptured. Tell me now, is that Love? Or is Love telling someone the truth?

Winter is coming, regardless of what we choose to believe, but the end of *this* story will not be quite so nice as the one in the fairy tale of the Grasshopper and the Ants.

You must make a choice as to which message you will believe.

Give a Portion to Seven

Give a portion to seven, and also to eight; for thou knowest not what evil shall be upon the earth.
Ecclesiastes 11:2

Now here's a thought for you. What if everything the doomsayers are saying really comes to pass and the coming years really bring economic chaos, and the world economy crashes? After all, the much-touted interdependence of a global economy doesn't seem to be working very well. We see economies failing around the world. Our multi-national corporations are scrambling for mergers that often result in failure. Our government's fiscal spending and debt are not exactly harbingers of hope and promise. And there are many economic gurus predicting a recession. Shall I go on?

If you knew for sure that you only had a couple of years of plenty left, what would you do with your resources today? Pharaoh was smart enough to listen to Joseph. How many warnings about dark times coming have we had from men of God today? Find soul-winning works of God that you know are bearing good fruit, and sow into them. Support them with everything you've got. Do all you can to help them prosper so they can get the Gospel out to lost souls while there's still time. Give a portion to seven, and also eight.

And if you don't have much money, then this is your golden opportunity to show your faith. God regards such sacrifices highly. There is no better time to show how much you really believe in the Gospel. The time may come when you have plenty of money, and the opportunity for such a sacrifice will be gone.

Be a good steward with your money, and be careful of mega-ministries that end every broadcast begging for money. Often, the desire for a bigger ministry can be a very subtle seduction that is not of the Lord. Don't be fooled by something just because it looks good and sounds holy. The Bible says that you'll *never* see the righteous begging bread.

We can store up canned goods and ammunition in little cabins in the woods, or we can sow into the one sure-fire thing that will see us through in time of great need. If there was ever a time to use our resources to sow mercy, it's now. We may not have that opportunity later.

And later is when we will so desperately need to reap that mercy that we have stored up

In a Dry Tree

For if they do these things in a green tree, what shall be done in the dry?

Luke 23:31

I've been doing some reading on what it was like in Germany during the years leading up to the Third Reich. There have been plenty of books written on why the German people allowed themselves to be taken over by the Nazis, but one of the things I've noticed is that the average person did not realize what was really coming until it was too late. They somehow felt that it would never really happen. Once the reign of terror was in place, however, they were trapped. The Nazis were a minority in the beginning, but were so well financed that they were able to overwhelm their opposition. They made it look like their ascension was inevitable and it was useless to resist.

Certainly there were other factors involved in the Nazi takeover of power, one of which, of course, was that the powers of Satan were marshaled behind them. So much so that many Christians looked at this as the establishment of the Antichrist.

This same scenario has worked itself out many other times throughout history. Average people never think it can happen. We have a tendency to feel that we are more civilized; times have changed, and it could never happen here. We let our guard down and open a door for Satan to get in.

I am not as politically motivated as some others are, but I do see the obvious connections. I look to the Word of God and see some woeful dark times coming upon the face of the earth. Do we think, as others have, that it could never happen to us? And yet, a quick read of Daniel and Revelation among other books shows that persecution is coming. Do we think like the people in Jeremiah's time and believe that we shall be delivered out of it all because God would never let that happen to us?

Many believe that we'll be raptured out of all this, but Scripture does not bear this out. Although we could argue, fuss, and debate this for hours, unless the people of God prepare themselves in the Lord, they will be in for some ugly surprises.

Just going to church does not make you a Christian. Finding a place of depth in God is where your strength comes from. The food you need to stockpile is in the Word of God. The ammunition and weapons needed come from taking a stand for the Gospel and winning lost souls to Christ. The place of refuge can only be found in the depth of the Spirit of God through fasting and prayer.

It has been said that the Christian you are today will be the one you are tomorrow. Now is the time to strengthen yourselves in the Lord. The Bible says there will be an hour of temptation that will come to try the whole world. Will you be ready, strong, and able to make a stand at that time? Are you making one today? If you're in the Spirit of the Lord, it won't matter.

Conversely, if you're *not* in the Spirit of the Lord, it won't matter either.

Lamentations

> *How does the city sit solitary that was full of people.*
>
> *Lamentations 1:1*

What if you could look out into the future and see the utter destruction of your people, but no one would listen to you no matter how loud you cried out? Consider how Jeremiah felt as he watched the Babylonians destroy Jerusalem, then carry away her people.

There had been a brief revival during Josiah's reign, but it had been superficial at best, because the Jews had gone right back into their carnal ways soon after Josiah's death. God could see into their hearts, and during that time of revival, had given Jeremiah repeated warnings of coming destruction.

Jeremiah had seemed like a crackpot to them at the time, but now he sat in the midst of the destruction of Mount Zion and mourned for the people of God. They just would not listen to the calls for repentance, because their hearts had run after messages of peace and prosperity and had trusted in the fact that they were God's chosen people.

The Jews trusted in their walls as a bulwark against the enemy of their souls, but those walls were broken down, and the enemy had entered into the sanctuary, because they were not built upon the righteousness of God. They trusted in brick and mortar instead of a heartfelt repentance before God. Shucks, they didn't even think they had been doing anything wrong.

I sincerely believe that we shall see another Babylonian captivity for the Mount Zion of today, the church of Jesus Christ. The scenario is just the same as in the day of Jeremiah – the messages we hear, the attitudes we've developed, the things we trust in for our salvation—and the warnings from God. I expect the results will also be the same.

That's a pretty harsh stand to take today when everyone trusts so much in their respective religions. Anyone who is out sounding an alarm of repentance in God's holy mountain looks like a crackpot—this hasn't changed either.

This time, however, we will face the great whore of Revelations, the modern-day Babylon. The Bible says that there will be an hour of temptation that will come to try the whole earth, and most people will submit to this ecumenical move toward a one-world religion.

Why? Because they have heard that God is Love, and He wants everyone to love each other so we can have religious peace.

> *For yourselves know perfectly that the day of the Lord so cometh as a thief in the night. For when they shall say, Peace and safety; then sudden destruction cometh upon them, as travail upon a woman with child; and they shall not escape.*
>
> *1 Thessalonians 5:2,3*

Believe me, it is coming. It's a lot closer than we would like to think. And it is written so that anyone who has ears to hear can hear.

The enemy is just outside the walls; the battle is set, yet so few see the danger.

Religious Intolerance

I heard on the BBC that the Southern Baptists have produced a book of prayers directed at the high and holy day of Hinduism. The prayers are, of course, directed to Baptists to pray for the conversion of the Indian people who are, as the booklet says, "lost in the darkness of Hinduism."

Pretty standard stuff, I'd say. But the hue and cry is that this is an extreme show of religious intolerance. One announcer went so far as to say that Jesus taught us to, "Do unto others as you would have them do unto you." In essence, they are calling for all religions to believe in each other so that we can all co-habitate in a "one world religion," but here the Baptists were being called hateful and insulting. "Shame on you Baptists! Baaad Baptists! Aren't we all supposed to love one another?"

If I were lost in Hinduism, however, I'd sure want somebody praying for me. Who wants to wake up in Eternity to find out you're going to Hell? What Jesus was really saying here was to have the guts to tell them the Truth. And the Truth, the Bible says, is an offense to the unsaved. Why is that?

Christianity is an exclusive faith. There is only one way to Heaven, and that is through Jesus Christ. Either that is the truth, or Jesus Christ was the biggest liar who ever lived. I know that when I felt the Spirit of God save my soul, there was absolutely no question that it was the only Truth on the face of the earth. Hinduism, however, is a bloodless cult that believes that there is a "many twined rope to heaven," and many of the "New Age" philosophies that have entered into our society today are based on these mystical religions.

Watch carefully as the ground swell of modern theological thought moves in the direction of one-worldism. Even supposed Christian leaders are leaning in this direction. To take a strong stand for the Gospel will someday be against the law and labeled as a "hate crime of intolerance."

You can be hated for lots of things. Just believing in Jesus Christ will not bring the persecution the Bible warns of to "every man that walks godly in Christ Jesus" in 2 Timothy 3:12. It is when you stand up and preach the Gospel to the lost and call for a repentance from sin—repentance, godly sorrow, Gospel basics, and holiness, not a tolerance for differences of opinion or lifestyle—that you will see persecution arise. If John the Baptist had just kept his mouth shut, he would have never had his head cut off!

And what does the Bible say?

> *...yea, the time cometh, that whosoever killeth you will think that he doeth God service.*
>
> *John 16:2*

When I see the mainstream media trying to use quotes from the Bible to justify demonic cults and move us into a one-world religion, then I figure that that time is coming soon. It's time to figure out which side you are on, and get ready to make a stand.

The Voice Said Cry!

The voice said, Cry. And he said, "What shall I cry?"

Isaiah 40:6

There are certain times when you can begin to feel a great movement in the Spirit of the Lord, like a great wind beginning to blow. You can sense it before you can feel it. Even animals can sense the oncoming of a storm. The pressure drops, the air becomes still, and an ominous feeling fills the air.

We are in such a time.

You can't quite put a finger on it, but you know that something is coming. You can feel it in your soul. So you look to the Word of God and you read the signs of the times.

If your attention is on the world around you, you will see prosperity, peace, and good times. People are scurrying to make their fortune so they can retire by the age of 30. Politicians are preaching a message of world peace and reconciliation. Economists tell us of how grand the outlook is. Televangelists tell us of how wonderful everything is going to be. There's nothing to worry about. Peace and safety they say, but down in the depths of your soul you sense a small nagging feeling that something is wrong.

If, however, your attention is focused on the Lord, there is an unmistakable ominous feeling in the air. When you turn to the prophets, you see a clear analogy of the times we are living in, and it scares you. So you turn to the Gospels, hoping to see something more soothing, and you see the same warnings for the times we are in right now. The Epistles aren't much better because they tell of a time coming when people will no longer endure sound doctrine. You don't dare turn to Revelations because the picture there is all too stark.

So you turn to the Lord in prayer, and He says, "Cry!" And you ask, "What shall I cry?" And the message is the same—a message of repentance to all.

There is no famine for the Word of God. It is for the *hearing* of the Word of God that Amos warned us about. The storm warnings are up for those who have eyes to see and ears to hear.

And yet He says, "Cry." "Sound an alarm in my holy mountain." (Joel 2:1)

The wind is picking up, and, as Bob Dylan once said, "you don't have to be a Weatherman to know which way the wind blows."

CHAPTER THREE

Revival

Four Steps to Revival

FOR REVIVAL TO HAPPEN, YOU FIRST HAVE TO REALIZE YOU NEED ONE. YOU HAVE to understand that "church as usual" is not enough. We need more. The Church does not thrive on complacency. Only a church that is on fire with the excitement of the Holy Ghost is alive. To get it, we must first find a place of repentance before God (for there is no real revival without Holy Ghost conviction and repentance). Anything else is merely a form of godliness and will fall somewhat short of the mark on the Day of Judgment.

Next, you then have to really *want* one. Like Rachel in Genesis 30:1, you have to want it more than life itself. You have to be willing to pay the price, whatever the cost, to see souls come to Salvation, and a Church that is overwhelmed with the Spirit of God. Much like a bride who is madly in love with her husband, so must we be desperate for the powerful presence of the Lord in every aspect of our lives and our church.

Then, we are ready to begin the third step of clamoring our way up to the Throne of God, to crash the holy gates, storm the holy of holies, not be denied, and claim a great and mighty move of God—and wait for Him to turn His golden scepter towards us. There is victory and power in God to those who will claim them, but there is also a price to pay.

The fourth step is the outpouring of the Holy Ghost and a harvest of lost souls, but He will only send these to those who are ready and who have paid the price to receive them. He will not send His precious souls to a people that do not care.

Revival and harvest are inseparable. Where you find one, you will find the other. We have seen great and mighty moves of God in the past, and there is no reason why we can't have one now. The only thing that holds back an outpouring of the Spirit of God is our lack of will.

Where is your local church at, friend? Is there an outpouring of the Holy Ghost? Are there souls getting saved everyday? Where's the fruit that God demands? Is there a physical manifestation of the Holy Ghost, a power so prevalent and thick that you can cut it with a knife? Are people being drawn to the Power and coming out transformed and on fire? Or are they finding a comfortable seat in a pew to be entertained every week?

It's one or the other. There are no shades of gray or levels of compromise with God.

Are you hungry for such a move of God? Perhaps it is time for us to look deeply at our churches and at ourselves and see what we have allowed ourselves to slide into.

Attitude for Revival

If my people, which are called by my name, shall humble themselves, and pray....

2 Chronicles 7:14

The book of Joel describes the spiritual conditions in these last days. In it, the Lord first describes a scene of spiritual desolation quite similar to the famine for hearing the Word of God that we see described in Amos 8:11. Jesus also spoke of this same spiritual dearth, as did Paul, and many other prophets of God. We don't hear this preached in the churches very often, but it is certainly written throughout the Word of God.

Once the Lord sets the scene in Joel, He then calls for the people of God to cry out to Him will all their heart with weeping and fasting, and for an outpouring of His Spirit to restore back us what we have lost spiritually. This is the blueprint from God to follow if we want to see a supernatural move of the Holy Spirit.

You see, we first have to realize that we don't have a real outpouring before we can *really* call out to God to send one. We then have to want one with all our hearts, and be willing to pay the price.

Revivals don't just happen; they don't fall out of the sky. Somebody has to be willing to go to the Throne with a repentant heart, and cry out to God. He is looking for those who not only are cut to the heart for lost souls, but who also have enough faith to literally storm the Throne for them. You can't sow seed into ground that has not been first prepared if you want to see a harvest

An old warrior in God once told me that the attitude God looks for is the one that will fight to the Throne of God and say, "I will not be denied! One of us is gonna move, and it ain't gonna be me!" That's the faith that moves mountains.

Allow me to make a challenge to those of you who really know God and want to see a revival. You say you want to see souls saved? You want to see a great and mighty move of God? It's time to fight for one—one that will rock the foundations of this ol' world.

I don't care what church you belong to, and neither does God. I'm not looking to start a church; I'm looking to see the ones we've got explode with the power of God. The Lord's waiting for those who have hearts that are willing to do whatever it takes in order to see this great promise of God be fulfilled, not somewhere else, but here.

Are you tired of "church as usual?" C'mon, let's make a difference that will be written into all eternity. Something that we'll be talking about 10,000 years from now, saying that we were there when the Holy Ghost crashed down and changed the lives of countless thousands of souls.

Famine

Woe to them that are at ease in Zion... but they are not grieved for the affliction of Joseph.

Amos 6:1,6

We are living in the days that have been prophesied just before the great and terrible day of the Lord comes. While we may see singing and dancing in our churches, the prophecies of the Word of God keep rolling on like a great stone wheel of judgment.

These are times of famine. We have all heard of some of the great moves of God in the past, and enjoy the retelling of stories of tremendous deliverance, of outpourings of the Holy Ghost that were as thick as fog, and of multitudes of souls coming down to the altars in deep, broken repentance. What wonderful stories! There are old-timers amongst us that remember, because they were present, but these are just stories to our generation.

The Book of Joel says that the Lord would cut off the corn, the wine, and the oil from the houses of joy, and Amos says that we would experience a famine for hearing the Word of God. Spiritual desolation has crept in upon us; we have a dry desert instead of the lush, blossoming fields of revival. This is what Paul spoke of when he said that, in the last days, Christians would no longer endure sound doctrine, but would heap up to themselves teachers that would preach unto them the smooth messages of love, peace and prosperity that their ears itch to hear. And they would turn their ears away from hearing the Truth. (2 Timothy 4:3)

Thus the famine. God said in Amos chapter 4 that He would rain upon one city and not the other, to make it evident that the Spirit of God is still real, but they still would not return to that deep walk in the righteousness of God.

These are the "perilous times" in the last days that the Bible warns us of in 2 Timothy 3:1. Religion becomes the most dangerous thing of earth when it leads to "church as usual"—a nice, easy-going gospel without the fear of God; without an understanding of Hell, and a resulting leanness of soul.

Only through repentance does a real move of God ever come. But our altar calls today have only become a calling together at the end of a wishy-washy message to hug each other and complain about all our problems. With all the churches in America, how many altar calls do we see for the lost? How many calls to repentance do we ever hear? And how many souls are cut to the heart with Holy Ghost conviction for an outpouring of the latter rain?

If this offends you, then let it lead you to storm the Throne of God like Nehemiah did for restoration of the Church of Jesus Christ to rise up in the Spirit of the Lord. The Church needs to storm the Throne of God for repentance and for one last great revival before it is all too late.

> *Woe unto you that desire the day of the Lord! To what end is it for you? The day of the Lord is darkness and not light.*
>
> *Amos 5:18*

Blow the Trumpet in Zion

Blow the trumpet in Zion, Zion.
Sound an alarm in my holy mountain....
(popular Christian song)

What an exciting song. We sing it with great gusto, but what does the rest of the passage in the Book of Joel have to say? What is this "alarm" all about?

Throughout the Prophets, the Gospels and epistles, we see warnings of a time of spiritual desolation coming upon the earth. In this century, we have seen exciting moves of God in many places around the world, and within the grasp of our memories is the evidence of what it is like to see an outpouring of the Spirit of God. Just a couple of generations ago, our churches were burning with a vibrancy that is still talked about today. Ask some of these old-timers what the Brush Arbor Revivals were like, and you can watch their eyes light up as they tell you.

In the last thirty to forty years, we've had a lot of good churches, but very few good revivals. Are we living in the time that the prophet Joel spoke about when the corn, the wine, and the oil have been withheld from the house of God? Is the excitement really gone?

There is a promise that is nested in the Scriptures that the Lord would raise up an army like none ever seen before. There is a time of restoration coming. I want to see this great outpouring of the Holy Ghost. I want to be there when the excitement runs through our streets like a river, and souls are running to the altar to receive the power of God in their lives. I believe it's coming and nothing will stop it.

But before it comes, there must be an alarm that is sounded. The trumpet must be blown in Zion to prepare for the battle and to call the people of God to cry out for Him to restore unto us that which the palmer worm and locust have eaten. No revival has ever come without somebody getting on their knees before God. Revival doesn't just drop out of the sky.

Are we satisfied with just "church as usual?" Then that is all we will have. Are you hungry for more? Then it is time to sound an alarm in God's holy mountain and prepare for the battle.

There's a rustling in the mulberry trees, and a breeze is beginning to blow. I can smell the smoke of battle afar off, and it is heading this way. What an exciting time to live in!

Salt of the Earth

Ye are the salt of the earth: but if the salt have lost his savour, wherewith shall it be salted?

Matthew 5:13

If you've ever participated in a real Holy Ghost revival, then you know there's a certain wind that fills your sails and drives you to an excitement within your soul that is unlike anything you've felt anywhere else. What is it that creates the excitement that fills your heart with joy and praise, and makes you want to reach to the heavens and give your whole life to God?

I've noticed that when I'm part of an outpouring like that, my personal problems melt away and are replaced with an overwhelming desire to serve the Lord and bring others to this salvation. Nothing else matters when I'm lifted up before God like that. My cup is overflowing, my life is blessed, and I'm are excited to be alive. This is the way life is meant to be—full of life, excitement, and zeal. That is the savour that is sent up to God.

But sometimes, life gets in the way and we tend to drift away and fall into a rhythm of "church as usual." We actually get to the place where we forget what it was like when we were ignited with the fire of God. How long has it been since we were so excited to go to church that we just couldn't wait to get there? We know the Truth of Jesus Christ, we go to church, we do all the right things; and yet, it just isn't the same, is it?

Sometimes, we drift so far away that we don't even realize how far we've gone, and we actually resent those whom the Lord sends to call us back to repentance. It is one thing to be entertained with interesting messages by our favorite preacher; it's something quite different to be inspired with the excitement of a Holy Ghost revival.

Oh, how wonderful it would be to see another outpouring of the Spirit of God running through our streets like rivers of fire! What would it take? What would we need to do to bring us back to that place of utter excitement?

We have to want it again. We have to desire it and mourn for it with all our hearts before God will listen and bring us back to that place again. Somebody has to get on their knees. Just like Daniel and Nehemiah did.

We are the salt of the earth, and we need a revival.

Rachel's Cry

Give me children or else I die.

Genesis 30:1

Rachel, like Hannah, couldn't stand the fact that she was barren. Their cry should also be the cry of every born again Christian today. How can we stand to be barren when the Lord has called us to bear forth much fruit?

First, we have to realize what we don't have before we can come to the point of Rachel's cry. Churches today do a good job of keeping the status quo and maintaining a place for those who are already saved to gather together to worship, but where are the great moves of God where thousands of souls throng to the altar for salvation? Where are the great healing ministries where the sick and afflicted come in great numbers to receive the manifestation of God's healing?

It's not enough just to have knowledge. Knowledge by itself "puffeth up" (1 Corinthian 8:1) Remember, there were two trees in the Garden, and if all you are interested in is analyzing the Word of God and figuring out prophecy, then you're barking up the wrong tree. The Word of God has to be received, and prophecy has to be revealed. You can know all kinds of theology and doctrine and not ever have revival or bear forth fruit.

Revival doesn't come from learning about it in a bible college study course. If that were the case, then with all the thousands of graduates every year from these bible colleges, you'd think we'd have revival sweeping the land.

But we don't. All we have is church.

Revival does not come cheap. There has to be such a heart-felt desire for the lost that we become willing to pay whatever price is necessary. If you don't have that deep overwhelming burden, you won't persevere in fasting and prayer all the way to the victory. You won't storm your way to the Throne of God to claim an answer no matter what. You have to demand an answer from God and not take "No" for an answer. You have to have the desperation of Rachel's cry.

Until the Lord starts to prepare people's hearts, all the works in the world will do little good. People have to have a hunger built in their hearts before they will receive the Truth, and only the Lord can do that. It's up to us to pray it in. Revival doesn't just fall out of the sky to a people who do not care enough to pray for it.

What if no one answers the call to pray? Then the Lord will give us a certain amount of time before He passes on to someone else. And when we will finally do stand before him, it will be without oil in our lamps, and we will think that He will know us because we've prophesied in His name. Instead, He will look us dead in the face and declare that He never knew us.

Ahhhhh. But for those who will pay the price, He will spread those great open arms with that wonderful smile, and say, "Well done, my good and faithful servant."

This is our time. Let's not let it pass us by.

Beside the Winepress of God

...and his son Gideon threshed wheat by the winepress....

Judges 6:11

At this time, Israel was going through a terrible persecution. The enemy had periodically destroyed the harvest so that the people of God were starving. People were hiding in caves and dens, and those who were not, were in fear for their lives. The judgments of God were heavy upon them because, instead of separating themselves from the idolaters of the land, they had embraced their pagan ways. The oppression had left them with little or no hope.

But Gideon was threshing his wheat by the winepress of God. That was the place where there was still hope to reap the Bread of Life. There was hope in that covered, hidden place in God. The Lord saw that hope and that's where the calling of God came.

The story of Gideon is one of the great victories of God. The Lord raised up someone who was little in his own sight to stand in the power of God and restore the presence and greatness of God in the land. What an incredible victory! Gideon leaned upon the Lord and trusted Him to bring about what flesh could never have accomplished.

There are warnings throughout the Word of God concerning the terrible spiritual desolation in the last days. We see it in Amos, Joel, Isaiah, Ezekiel,

Revelations, Thessalonians, to just name a few. Even Jesus warned us about it.

Although we read in our church bulletins about wonderful things that are happening, we still remain hungry and starving for a great move of God in our churches. Where are the glories that we have heard about in the revivals of times past? As it says in James 2:26, "...the body without the spirit is dead," and so are we in our own time of spiritual desolation. The enemy has destroyed the harvest and sucked the faith and hope out of us for the restoration of a great and mighty outpouring of God. We remain sedate and satisfied with what we've got, and begin to believe that this is all God has for us.

But there are those who plow their hope into the ground beside the winepress of God. We huddle close to the place where the Spirit of the Lord is pressed out and look to the heavens for the increase. Surely, the Lord has not forgotten His people.

There comes a time when you have had enough of the oppression, when you're tired of being second-rate in society, when you're sick and tired of being comfortable with a dead church, and when you are ready to stand for the honor of God regardless what the cost may be.

When the Lord raises up His ministers to burn a fire of defiance, there will always be resistance, but the Lord knows those who are willing to stand in the power of God to proclaim victory and deliverance. When the fire of God is flowing through your veins, there is nothing that can stop you. And once the fire is kindled, it will grow into a blaze that will consume every enemy that stands in the way.

"Send down an outpouring of the Holy Ghost, O Lord that will shake the very foundations of the earth! Lord, we claim victory!"

Thresh beside the winepress of God, come what may, and believe God for the greatest revival of all time—for it will surely come.

Just the Time for a Prophet

And Elijah the Tishbite, who was of the inhabitants of Gilead, said unto Ahab, As the LORD God of Israel liveth, before whom I stand, there shall not be dew nor rain these years, but according to my word.

1 Kings 17:1

And just when things were getting comfortable for them!

Everything was going so well. Why does the Lord always seem to send someone to upset the applecart just when we have gotten our lives organized and we don't have to strive as hard anymore?

We work hard at packaging up our religion so that it will roll along on autopilot. All the hard stuff has been accomplished; all the persecution has been overcome; all the work has been done to get us to this place of security. And now that we have "arrived," we should be able to take it easy for a while.

A friend of mine commented once that people *love* religion. Why? Because it is so easy! We get to a point where all the hard work is done, and we can rely on the system to make all the decisions now. All we have to do is go to church and be a member in good standing. We do the good works, the canned food drives, and the basket socials. We're covered. We can relax and be raptured. But there is no heart-rending cry to God for revival.

These are the times when the Lord raises up prophets to turn our complacency upside down. As one friend said, "they come to comfort the afflicted, and afflict the comfortable." The prophet, as Leonard Ravenhill once said in *Picture of a Prophet*, "Is a man who is rejected by other men, even other good men, because they consider him too austere, too severely committed, too negative and unsociable." They never bring forth the message that we want to hear; only the message that we need to hear. That characteristic is the thing that keeps them from being popular—at least in *their* lifetime.

But that is the thing that makes them popular with God; they are men who fear God and nothing else. People who are only concerned with what the Lord thinks of them are not concerned with what the world thinks. They can't. They are under an edict from God to tell people the Truth, declare unto Israel (i.e. the Church) their sin, and bring them back to repentance.

The Lord rarely raises up prophets from those who are well-known and have national prominence. You'd think that, if He did, then people would stand up and take notice. But the Lord raises up His prophets out of nowhere so that you will listen to the message, not the messenger.

If there was ever a time we needed one of those old-fashioned prophets of God, it is now. It hasn't rained in a while, and we need an outpouring. Before it rains, however, we, as the people of God, have got to come to that place of repentance before Him and cry out for revival.

We need one badly. And this would be just the time for the Lord to send one.

Church of the Laodiceans

I have need of nothing.... - the church of the Laodiceans,

Revelations 3:17

Frank Bartleman, an early leader of the Pentecostal movement at the Azusa Street Revival, said in his book *Azusa Street*, "A revival almost always begins among the laity. The ecclesiastical leaders seldom welcome reformation. History repeats itself. The present leaders are too comfortably situated as a rule to desire innovation that might require sacrifice on their part. And God's fire only falls on sacrifice. An empty altar receives no fire!"

Is it any different today? Do any of us look back to the times when our churches were aflame with the outpourings of the Holy Ghost? When "normal" church life meant nights full of prayer, and the resulting manifestations of signs and wonders, supernatural healings, and gifts of the Spirit? Can we look back to a time when meetings lasted for hours and the congregations were so enveloped in the glory of God that no one bothered watching the clock? What happened to our concept of "church?"

I have listened, more times than I can count, to people who have asked me where can they go to church to feel that kind of anointed power? Where can they go to get fed? They are starving for something more in God, and can't find it where they are now. And yet there was a time, generations ago, when their church was on fire for God.

Now, however, our church leaders give us excuses, or worse, we are told about some program that the church is going to purchase that will help us gain the "unchurched."

Here's a clue: There will be no outpouring from God that will come from some sophisticated, theologically correct program that is plucked from the Tree of Knowledge. Revival has to burn in our hearts before it can ever flow in our churches, and only deep, prevailing prayer will set those hearts aflame for something more in God than what they are getting in their dead church.

Do you throw yourself down before the Throne of God, broken-hearted for the lost and for a church that no longer feels the need for a revival? Are you grasping the horns of the altar with the determination of Rachel's cry, "Give me souls lest I die?" Are you willing to storm the Throne of God with all boldness, demanding a move from God? Does your heart cry out to the point that you are determined to plant yourself before Him and refuse to take "No" for an answer?

Or are you like the church of the Laodiceans – satisfied with their church, lukewarm and comfortable.

The Lord will give the churches a certain space of time to repent, then He will raise up stones in their place. Just like He always does.

Three Wise Women

It has been said that, if the three wise men at the Nativity had been three wise women, they would have asked directions, arrived on time, cleaned the stable, helped deliver the baby, and given practical gifts. I reckon so. But the Lord didn't do it that way, did He?

Of course, had it been one of us men, we would have probably booked a room in the King David Hotel, ordered a gift from Amazon.com, and hired the best of physicians to be at the bedside.

Funny how God works in ways we would never have figured, but He always gets incredible results. Who would have ever thought that He would choose a stable for the birth of His son? Yet from this humble place, God chose to change world history.

When the Lord decides to do something, He often moves in ways that the carnal mind would never have chosen. To bring about His purposes, He needs yielded vessels to carry out the work, not sophisticated intelligent men. When we try to figure out how we will accomplish what has been set before us, we too often end up with something that may look good, but does not carry the same eternal weight that it would have, if only we had allowed Him to lead us.

We purchase programs with sets of instructions, plan out campaigns, take surveys, place ads, and pursue anything else that we think will bring about the desired responses. God, on the other hand, chooses foolish things to confound the wise. He calls His prophets out of nowhere, raises up on-fire preachers with unpopular messages, and relies on the prayers of people who are just simple enough to believe Him. But if God's work is going to be accomplished, it has to be Him who makes it work.

I believe that the Lord desperately wants to move in our communities in such a mighty way that it would rattle our teeth and shake the very foundations of our denominational traditions. Will He find willing, yielded vessels ready to answer the call? Or are we too comfortable and willing to settle in our churches and allow the ecclesiastical hierarchy set the pace?

If you want something different than what you've got, then you've got to do something different than what you've done. There is a price to be paid. Revival doesn't come unless somebody gets down on their knees.

When it comes, don't be surprised if it is like nothing you've ever seen before.

That is, of course, unless you've got a better plan.

CHAPTER FOUR

Admonition to the Churches

Two Paths; Two Trees

CHURCH LEADERSHIP HAS THE MOST INFLUENCE ON THE BODY OF CHRIST. THEY can also do the most damage by resisting a move of God, therefore the Lord always appeals to them first in preparation for any great move of God.

We are at one of those times now. Spiritually, the ground is fallow, dry, and hard. It is time now to break up that fallow ground. The rain is coming and, when it comes, it will be a deluge, but the ground must be prepared first. We are at a focal point, a fork in the road of sorts, where we will decide for ourselves and for our society which path we will take. We will either be satisfied with church as usual, content that we have "taken care" of the religious aspects of our life; or we will recognize how dry we are, and not be satisfied until we have an outpouring of the Holy Ghost like has never been since the beginning of time.

Throughout Church history, there have always been two forces at work. Countering a sharp, focused evangelical fire, there is always a move to slow down the pace and be "normal." On one hand, we have the fiery prophets interested only in exposing the raw truth. On the other, we have the pastoral influence to protect the sheep and to keep them from being offended and lost. Either one, taken to an extreme and excluding the other's influence, will not have any long lasting results.

The old brush arbor revivals have often been portrayed as an example of extreme "hellfire and brimstone" preachers who have offended more souls than they won. At least that's what Hollywood would have us to believe. On the contrary however, thousands of souls were saved and transformed, churches were revived and started, ministries were ignited, and the fabric of our nation was changed.

True, many were offended and blamed the strong preaching as an excuse, but many more were not. They had seen Jesus, had felt the Spirit of God, and had gone on to serve the Lord.

But Bible colleges and seminaries, worried about rashness in the past, began to counsel their students to hold back from that kind of preaching. The idea was that it is too easy for every would-be and self-styled prophet to raise himself up to hammer the rest of us with condemnation.

So we began to transform the Gospel into a religion. An ecclesiastical structure was built as a framework to hang the Gospel on, and a more "socially responsive" church began to be formed. Every denominational religion has evolved in this manner.

The problem is that, in becoming more educated, we've lost the fire of being driven by the Spirit of God; instead, we have filtered everything through a sophisticated lens. We have become more directed by prepared messages, sociological programs and psychological approaches than by the leading of the Holy Spirit.

Jesus and all the prophets didn't seem the least worried about offending the wicked, but our pulpits today are sanitized from such offensive preaching and are more concerned with convincing people of God's love.

There is a subtle and yet very important difference. It is the same as the difference between the two trees in the Garden of Eden.

Blood, Fire, Fear, and Souls of Men

There are four indicators that, although not conclusive or all-embracing, show the depth of any ministry. These are Blood, Fire, Fear, and Souls. They may not embody the total essence of Christianity, but without these elements, a ministry shows a lack of wisdom, understanding, and authority in God.

When you're wondering what's missing as far as power and depth and strength in a particular ministry, look to see if these elements are present. You will often find that when a church places its emphasis on other things instead of these essentials, that ministry will seem to be running out of gas. Their candle is flickering, their oil is about to run out, and they are sliding into the same category of "church" that the old prophets clamored against. They may be comfortable as far as their stand in the community goes, but, if I may so say, there is no comfort in being lukewarm.

Let me explain what I mean by these four elements.

Blood

When there is no strong pronouncement in actual words of the Blood of Jesus, there is a lack of spiritual understanding of the power that is in that Blood, and also concerning the powers of darkness. Satan cannot stand even the mention of the Blood of Jesus. It is a prime weapon in our warfare.

I have heard and read sinners' prayers that don't even mention being washed in that Blood. I have been in services where it has not ever been mentioned. Have we forgotten that it was only the Blood of Jesus that won redemption? Victory came through the Blood of Jesus Christ. It is the very thing that defeated Satan once and for all, and the one thing that he cannot stand against.

It has been said that if you know God, you will know the devil, and, if you don't know the devil, you don't know God. Never underestimate the enemy. We are in a fierce war and if we are not aware of it at all times, we will be seduced into a deadly slumber.

In order for us to gain the complete and total victory over sin, we have to remain covered in the Blood. We may hear the words "the Blood of Jesus" in our churches, but what we need to emphasize is the dramatic importance of the power of those words.

Remember, we are in enemy territory, and he thinks we're trespassing.

Fire

When I speak of fire, I am not referring to fire in our souls, but the presentation of a true picture of Hell.

Hell is a real place—a terrible place. We didn't create it, but it is most definitely there. So why do we try to smooth it over with expressions like a "Christless Eternity" or "separation from God" and other such socially acceptable phases? Consider for a moment that Hell is the most prevalent reality there is because most people, according to the Word of God, are going to wind up there.

God commanded Ezekiel to *warn* the wicked of their ways, yet we try to persuade them with a nicer approach so that we don't offend them. God has said that it is by the fear of the Lord that men depart from evil, but many tell us that it is by the "love" of God, because that is what they've been taught to believe.

Once again we see the allure of the Tree of the Knowledge of Good and Evil in the Garden of Eden by the fact that we are often led by what we want to hear and, as a result, by what we have figured out—not by the depth of the Spirit and the Word of God.

Our great revivals in the past have shown us that when people realize the reality of Hell, then Holy Ghost conviction will bring them to the Cross in great numbers. Even today, when we see plays such as "Heaven's Gates and Hell's Flames" we see multitudes of people come to the altar to repent because the reality of an eternity in hell has gripped their souls.

In too many cases, however, we return to our old comfortable ways soon after the presentation is over. Why? Is it because we think that is an old-fashioned gospel? But since when has God changed His message? We consider this a more modern age, so our churches today have a very different approach, a different message, and, predictably, very different results.

If that is not so, then where is the fruit, the reaping of lost souls? How many people were saved at your church last week? How about last month? I'm not talking about Christians coming down to the altar week after week for the same old things that they can never seem to get the victory over. And I'm not talking about an increase in church membership from the dead wood of some other dead church. I'm talking about lost souls coming under Holy Ghost conviction and coming to a place of repentance before God, then surrendering their hearts and souls to Him. That's the fruit that churches are supposed to be bearing.

Remember that the Lord cursed the fig tree for not having fruit on it, even though it was not in season. There are no excuses.

Fear

We see an emphasis on a "love gospel" in many churches today. The fear of God is minimized and often villanized for scaring people. 1 John 4:18 says "perfect love casteth out all fear" but the Lord was not contradicting himself. The Fear of God is the foundation upon which everything else rests.

There is no love without fear, because love is the keeping of God's commandments (2 John 1:6), which is impossible without the fear of the Lord. The Word of God says that it is by the fear of the Lord that men depart from evil (Proverbs 16:6).

Wisdom, the "principal thing," *is* the fear of the Lord (Job 28:28). According to Isaiah 11:3, it made Jesus of quick understanding and will do the same for you. Jesus was heard because he feared (Hebrews 5:7). The fear of God actually gives you strong confidence (Proverbs 14:26). Satanic fear is has no place in you when you have the holy boldness that only comes through the fear of God.

Lest we succumb to a sophisticated definition of the word fear, remember that Moses' knees smote together from the fear of God. David, the "apple of God's eye," feared God so much that the flesh on his bones trembled, as did Paul's. The great prophets of God spoke of the fear of the Lord in terms of "dread." This is not the "awesome respect" that we hear our ecclesiastical scholars and preachers speak of today.

If the fear of God is so important according to the Scriptures, why is it not emphasized in our churches? Is it because it is not a comfortable message, and we would rather hear about "smooth" things?

If we do not preach a strong Gospel, we will not have a strong congregation, and our parishioners will not have the strength to stand in the day of temptation that is coming to try the whole earth. Like it or not, the dark days of spiritual famine are coming and we will need the strength that comes from a strong stand in the depth of the Spirit to make it through those times. That comes from a walk with God that is strengthened and driven by the Fear of Him.

Don't be fooled by a popular "Love Gospel." The Word says to "behold the goodness *and* the severity of the Lord."

Souls of Men:

The great focus of our churches today is on ourselves. We are so enamored with our own spiritual needs, that we have forgotten our first love.

Altar calls for the lost have been replaced with pity lines for church members to get prayed over for everything from a sore foot to a new job. I see people coming to the altar for prayer for the same troubles week after week, but never able to get the victory, never able to overcome, never able to receive the strength to stand.

All the while, souls are dropping off into an eternity in Hell with no hope of ever getting out, and no one is cut to the heart. We say we are, but talk is cheap. Real faith is action.

I learned a long time ago that when you have problems, go take care of someone else's problems and yours will dissipate into thin air. How many of us are storming the Throne of God for the lost? How many of us are taking the battle to the streets and witnessing our hearts out? Where are the old-fashioned warriors of old? The ultimate goal of Christianity is to win souls. When we lose sight of that, we lose our focus on God and we lose our power in Him.

There was a time when these attributes could be found in almost any church, but no longer. We've become homogenized and sophisticated and intelligent—and lifeless. By definition, homogenization and sophistication mean to take the raw elements out of a product and to refine it so that it is more palatable to the consumer.

This works great for food, but not for the soul.

Ruth

> *...And when Boaz had eaten and drunk, and his heart was merry, he went to lie down at the end of the heap of corn: and she came softly, and uncovered his feet, and laid her down.*
>
> *Ruth 3:7*

What a picture of humility Ruth was! The Book of Ruth is full of analogies of God's dispensation to the Gentiles, and of His overall plan of salvation. Just as the Lord uses the image of a woman as His analogy for His Bride, so we see a picture in Ruth of the perfect church of the New Covenant.

In Ruth, we see a Gentile who has left her people and her gods to follow her Jewish mother-in-law back to Israel. Willing to work in the harvest fields of the Lord, gleaning amongst the sheaves for souls, and asking nothing for herself in return, she presents to us a picture of purity, humility, and service. But there is something more to her story.

Who wouldn't fall in love with this woman? There is something beautiful in her that comes through the pages, something beyond the actual text that gives you a feel for this woman's heart and the purity of her soul. She is not just the picture of a perfect woman; she shows the very essence of Christ and is the very image of the Christian church.

Here is a woman who not only willingly gave up her own personal life to serve in the harvest fields, but she also went so far as to lay her life down at the feet of her master. She gave her all in unselfish service to the Lord. She was Charity incarnate—the giving of oneself out of love to the service of God and the winning of souls.

In laying her life down in perfect, selfless humility, she made possible the great redemptive Plan of God. What a sense of great celebration we see as the story comes to an end! As Naomi holds her grandson, we feel the wonderful resolution to all that she has gone through. God had brought Israel back to Himself through Ruth. Redemption, restoration, and rejoicing! What a story!

I can't wait to be there when the culmination of the real story, of which Ruth was an analogy, finally plays itself out in the Kingdom of Heaven. Let us all strive to see in our own hearts and lives the very essence of Ruth so that we also may be able to partake in the Marriage Supper of the Lamb.

What a celebration it will be!

Perspective

Every way of a man is right in his own eyes: but the LORD pondereth the hearts.

Proverbs 21:2

Perspective. Everybody's got one. That's why everyone thinks what they believe in is right. Let's face it, if you didn't believe you were right, you wouldn't believe that way—right? So what about everyone else? Oh, if only they could see things the way you see them, then they would understand. (Or is it the other way around?)

In the scientific community, you start with a basic premise and set about proving it. But when the facts show evidence to something contrary, a good scientist will follow that lead in hopes of discovering the truth. There is no deep, profound assault on his ego by changing his premise—merely an opportunity to switch to the correct path and perhaps discover something worthy of a Nobel Prize.

In matters of the heart and soul, however, we have a tendency to establish what we have decided to believe, and then accept evidence that proves our beliefs. Anything that points to something contrary is often times ignored, dismissed, or rationalized to minimize its significance. We hold on to the beliefs that have found root in our hearts and souls, and will fiercely defend them.

In other words, we will believe what we want to believe in spite of the facts.

Sometimes, the things that we believe are a result of pondering the facts and coming to a rational conclusion, but often they are not. More often than not, our belief system is based on the ideals, social mores, and beliefs that we have inherited from childhood. We don't always know why we believe them—we just do. And even when it is something that we have figured out for ourselves, we are loath to let it go. It would mean admitting we are wrong.

The heart of man is very deep, the Bible says, and is hard to understand. When it pertains to an idea in our minds, we can switch our position easily; but when it involves a belief that pertains to morals, desires of our hearts, and something that has been planted in our souls, we resist every effort to change—in spite of the facts, even in spite of the Word of God. It takes the active, living, Spirit of God to deal with our hearts in order to change us.

That is why it is so desperately important for men of God to preach only under the anointing and the Spirit of God. "Life and death is in the power of the tongue."

And that is also why a church that is dead to the Spirit is so lethal to a human soul (Ephesians 5:11).

The Sands of Sinai

And the manna ceased on the morrow after they had eaten of the old corn of the land; neither had the children of Israel manna any more; but they did eat of the fruit of the land of Canaan that year.

Joshua 5:12

What a feeling that must have been for the Israelites! They had finally made it! All those years in the desert. All those years in bondage! They were home, finally home. Five hundred years ago, they had left as a small family, and now had finally returned as a nation of millions.

What a journey it had been—hundreds of years of horrible slavery and bondage had finally been broken by a prophet of God. They had walked through the Red Sea, and had entered into that long, dry walk through the desert.

They were so close to the Promised Land that they could practically smell it. They could almost taste the milk and honey they were told about. It was so close, so close! They were almost there…

The sands of the Sinai desert have hundreds of thousands of unmarked graves in it. The bodies that lay there had once seen the great judgments of God on the heathen, the incredible miracles at the Red Sea and in the desert. They had seen Mount Horeb smoke and rumble with the presence of God, and had heard His voice. They had received His Commandments and had made a covenant with the Almighty. They knew what the righteousness of God was, but they had succumbed to the lusts of their own flesh and hearts. And they had died in the wilderness.

Their hearts ached for the Promised Land, but they believed they would inherit it simply because they were God's chosen people. They were not willing to walk in the ways of God to get there. Because they had chosen to walk in their own ways, all they inherited was sand.

The Bible says through much tribulation we enter into the kingdom of God. It is not because God is not willing or able, but because we have a tendency to walk after our own ways, and refuse the ways of God. Every excuse to dodge the righteousness of God helps dig your grave in Sinai. Either you have a love for righteousness, or you don't; you will either find a way to overcome sin, or you will make an excuse for it.

You may have crossed the Red Sea, but if you want to cross over Jordan, you will have to do it God's way. If you will yield to the Spirit of God, He will give you all the power you need, but if you won't, then neither will He.

The ones who did cross Jordan entered into a new promise and hope of redemption that their Fathers only dreamed of. In the ages to come, will you be one of those who claimed the victory and crossed over to that long awaited land of milk and honey? Or will you trust in your own ways and end up with the wind whipping the sands of time over your grave—so close to the Promised Land, so close, and yet so far away.

Where Shall Wisdom Be Found?

...but where shall wisdom be found?

Job 28:12

Mankind has always struggled with truth, reality, and existence, and philosophers and religions have always abounded with answers.

Just looking up into the evening sky fills mankind with questions. How big is the universe? Is God really up there? What really happens when you die? What is the real truth? Which is the right way?

Someone once tol d me that there are over 60,000 different religions in the world. I'm not surprised. Then, there are innumerable spiritual philosophies, from New Agers to witches. Add to that the number of different ideologies that are atheistic, like communism, psychiatry, and secular humanism, and you've got more on your plate than you can handle. But where shall wisdom be found?

If it were left up to us to just make a good guess, then God would not be righteous in judgment. After all, how would you really know if you had guessed correctly? And how could you be judged if there was no way of really knowing whether you were wrong?

But the Lord has not left us without a way to know the truth.

Making a good guess, or picking a number out of the hat is not the point. You can be satisfied with whatever choice you make if that is all you are searching for, but God looks for those who have a love of righteousness. He is a holy God, and in order to worship Him, you have to love holiness. Otherwise, you are just going through the motions of making a choice that you think sounds good.

The point isn't to pick a theory that suits you, but to search for righteousness and holiness. The love of righteousness has to resonate in your soul for you to even want to find it. Jesus said, "My sheep hear my voice, and another they will not follow." (John 10:27)

When you find a church that is planted deeply in the ways of God, you will find a place that resounds with the Spirit of God, a witness to the truth. There is a power that can be felt, a feeling in the air, and knowledge deep in your soul that this is really the truth. Your head may follow it's own ego, but your soul will know the truth.

Whether you choose to follow your head and the things you would like to believe, or submit to what your soul tells you is right, the choice that you make will determine your eternal destiny.

Where is wisdom, then?

> *And unto man he said, "Behold, the fear of the Lord, that is wisdom; and to depart from evil is understanding."*
>
> *(Job 28:28)*

Desperate Prayer

It is said that prayer changes things. One of the things it changes is the person that's doing the praying.

Deep prayer changes you deeply. A little prayer only changes you a little. Although there are several instances in the Bible of some fairly short prayers, the men that were praying were not guilty of quick, light-hearted approaches to God. These men were warriors who were used to laboring before the Throne of God, sometimes night and day, to claim their victory. Great and mighty answers from God do not come cheaply.

Prayer is the backbone of a Christian's life, and you can tell how much time someone spends in the prayer room by what he is like outside the prayer room. Everything seems to be quick and fast these days—from the food we eat to the business we conduct—but that time-honored wrestling in prayer is not something that can ever be capsulated into a quick, easy-to-use package.

You may be too busy to spend deep hours on your knees now, but you will reap the consequences for a long, long time. Just as sure as you get what you pay for here in this life, so it is with your relationship with God. Be careful, my friend: If you brush Him aside for a more convenient time, He might do the same with you.

A friend of mine once said that true honor comes when the Lord not only hears your prayers—but answers them. That is true honor! Spending fifteen minutes with God will get you neither power, nor favor, nor honor with Him. What it does give you, however, is a false assurance that you are OK with Him. You prayed all right, but did you contend before the Throne of Grace until you broke through and got your answer? Did you wrestle with Him until you won the victory? The prayer warriors in the Bible did. You see, there really wasn't anything more important in their lives than their time spent with God.

In the church world today, I hear more emphasis placed on going to church than on going to the Throne of God. I believe Church is good, but, as Keith Green once said, going to church doesn't make you any more a Christian than going to McDonald's makes you a hamburger. You can't just package up your faith in a box, tie a bow around it, place it on a shelf and think you will pass muster with God because you went to church on Sunday. You will end up like the five foolish virgins in Matthew 25 that had no oil in their lamps.

In order to have a great and mighty move of God, the people who know Him will have to humble themselves in deep, prevailing prayer to cry out for a revival. It takes the desperate prayer of a man or woman of God—someone who will not be denied—to bring down the fire of the Holy Ghost.

It can happen right now like it has never happened before. Can you picture such an outpouring of the Spirit that hundreds, even thousands, of souls would be giving their hearts to the Lord every single day? Can you picture a revival that starts here, then sweeps throughout the world? It can happen. But you've got to want it more than life itself.

You've got to want it enough to pray.

Pecan Pie

Blessed be the God of Shadrach, Meshach, and Abednego, who hath sent his angel, and delivered his servants that trusted in him, and have changed the king's word, and yielded their bodies, that they might not serve nor worship any god, except their own God.

Daniel 3:28

Those three Hebrew children feared God more than they feared King Nebuchanezzar, and were more concerned about burning in hell than burning in that furnace. They trusted that God would deliver them, but even if He didn't, they were not going to compromise with a worldly religion, even if it meant their lives. They were willing to yield their bodies to pay whatever price needed.

Where did their strength come from that gave them such courage for God? What persuaded them that their place in God was better than whatever the world had to offer? Throughout time, men and women have been willing to sacrifice all to stand and fight for the honor of God because they had a taste of the real thing, and would not compromise for the cheap imitation that the world and its social religion has to offer.

It's kinda like pecan pie.

Did you ever sink your teeth into Grandma's home baked Pecan pie and felt like you could just fall into it? She'd spend hours on the crust, cooking up the pecans, adding that special touch to make it come out just right. And she'd serve it absolutely free, with all the love in her heart.

And then you stop by a convenience store and you see these little pecan pies for 49¢. It's got real pretty packaging, great marketing and presentation. And convenient? Shucks. All packaged up and ready to go. How easy! And they're everywhere! Seems like you can pick up these pre-packaged pecan pies just about anywhere you go. Corporations have spent millions to figure out how to cook these things. They've got educated guys with real certificates and degrees that show smart they are and that they can cook up these pies real good. And a whole pile of equipment to work with!

How on earth did Grandma ever think she could cook up something as good as these big-time, smooth organizations? But, by golly, all that those professionals could produce with all their sophistication was merely an imitation of Grandma's real thing.

Many of the big church organizations of today are like those big companies that only offer an imitation of the real thing. Their sophistication and size may seem to offer what you would find in a real move of God, but something is missing. They are packaged professionally to look good, and have great marketing to sell it well, but it's just not the same as the real thing. There is a difference.

Once you've had a taste of a real outpouring of the Holy Spirit in your church, nothing else will do. It's not about fancy packaging, slick marketing or how professionally it has been organized. It is that special ingredient that can only come from the Throne of God. Just like Grandma's pie, there's something real about it that just cannot be imitated or duplicated by even our best carnal efforts.

That special ingredient is the Spirit of the Lord. That is what gave the three Hebrew children the strength to make the stand that they did. Their confidence and boldness to face a fiery furnace didn't come from an empty faith in a packaged religion. Neither did it come because someone had simply told them that God was real. They had touched the Throne of God themselves and had tasted of the real thing, and that was enough for them to face even death if need be.

Are you hungry for the *real* thing, not the same old stuff you getting from church? Do you want something that will reach deeper in your soul than a superficial religious belief in God? Does your heart cry out for a substance and reality in your faith that cannot be found by going through the motions on Sunday morning?

There *is* a real thing that can satiate the desperate hunger in your soul. It was bought and paid for by the Blood of Jesus Christ and is offered freely to all those who reach out and call for it.

When the Spirit of God enters your church and flows through the congregation, it transforms the lives of everyone there. It brings life to the deadness of religion, excitement to mundane church services, brightness to dull traditions, fire to cold faith, and a drive and desire to serve the Lord for the rest of your life. You will never settle for a cheap imitation again.

And like Grandma's pecan pie, man, does it taste good!

How good? Man, it's to die for!

Where Are the Nine?

And one of them, when he saw that he was healed, turned back, and with a loud voice glorified God, and fell down on his face at His feet, giving him thanks: and he was a Samaritan.

Luke 17:15,16

A friend of mine told me that she would rather go witnessing up in the Northeast where at least people know they need salvation, than to be here in the midst of the Bible Belt where so many people—no matter how much they are in sin—only ***think*** they are saved. That's a pretty tough statement, but if you think about it for a moment, you will realize the truth of it.

Have we become so comfortable with our salvation that we have forgotten to turn around and give thanks? There were ten lepers that were healed, but only one turned back to give glory to God. Do we rest in the fact that, because we go to church on Sunday, we can now relax because that part of our lives is now taken care of, and we can now go on to other more important facets of our lives?

Of course, most everyone would take issue with that statement. After all, we go to church and have been saved, and believe in God, and we go to church, and we know the Truth, and we believe we are saved, and we go to church, and... and... and... Well, after all, we *do* go to church...and we *do* believe, don't we?

I mean, really, what else do you want? Read the Bible? Well, we read the Bible…sometimes. And we pray … when we need to. We keep most of the commandments—at least the ones we need to, and God understands that we can't keep them all … doesn't He?

Have we forgotten something here? Are we missing something? Or can we just relax, and be raptured? After all, we do go to church…

If you have the chance, talk to an old-timer who remembers the old brush arbor revivals, and ask him what it was like. Or, find a missionary who has come back from some Third World country and ask him or her what it is like to witness where people are so hungry for God that they implore you for more.

Now, take a handful of Gospel tracts, go stand on a corner, pass them out, and see the difference.

Jesus asked, "Where are the nine?" I've got a hunch that they are a lot closer to home than we think.

Passing on the Glory

We will not hide them from their children, showing to the generation to come the praises of the Lord, and his strength, and his wonderful works that he hath done...That they might set their hope in God, and not forget the works of God, but keep his commandments.

Psalm 78

Oh, the Glory! Have you ever experienced the outpouring of the Holy Ghost filling up services with His Shekinah Glory? Do you remember when God came down, and hearts were overwhelmed, and praises poured out from hearts that were open? When souls were filled to overflowing and the Spirit of God flowed like anointing oil through our hearts? Souls were saved, people were healed, and multitudes were drawn to the fountain of life pouring out from the Throne.

Where has all of this gone? What happened to the great moves of God that we once experienced in our churches? Those who should have passed on the glory to the next generation have instead given us over to man-made doctrines, to secular preaching, and to churches that have lost their vibrancy. Preachers with depths in God have been turned into to educated theologians who know so much doctrine about God that they no longer know what it's like to be led of the Spirit.

If that is not so, then where is the manifestation of the Power of God?

The Kingdom of God is not in word, but in power. But our churches have turned the Gospel of Jesus Christ into just another religion. Lost souls that are desperate for God have looked upon Christianity as just another philosophy, another dead religion with no power, no Spirit, and no glory.

Their cry is "Sir, we would see Jesus!" We crave a demonstration of the Spirit and power. Let Holy Ghost conviction open our hearts to return to that place in God that we once had.

Church "as usual" is death, and we need Life! That can only come from men of God who are not afraid to take a stand for righteousness and for the fear of God. Only those who are willing to walk the walk of the lowly Nazarene and allow their lives to be filled with the power of God instead of theology can lead us to a restoration of what we have lost.

The indictment stands against those who remember, but have not had the guts to pass it on.

Mahershalalhasbaz

...and she conceived, and bare a son. Then said the Lord to me, "Call his name Mahershalalhashbaz."

(Isaiah 8:3)

And for a nickname?

One thing's for sure. There won't be any other kids in his class with the same name. You won't find this one in those little books of what to name your baby.

I sometimes wonder what ever happened to Maher... whats-his-name. His father, Isaiah, had a pretty tough job, and they lived at some very tumultuous times. It has been said that they finally killed Isaiah by boiling him in oil. How did that affect Mahershalalhashbaz? With a name like that he surely stood out in the crowd, but did he stand up *against* the crowd? Did he inherit the strength and faith of his father?

How about Job's kids? The Bible says that, at the end, he had seven sons and three daughters. (There go the keys to the car!) Did they understand what Job had gone through to establish the sovereign authority of God?

After all, they were only there during the times of Job's blessings. They never experienced his times of adversity.

Isaac and Rebecca had their problems with kids, too. Esau had taken a couple of wives that the Bible says were grievous to them. Was this just another case of problems with the in-laws? Or perhaps their first-born son just didn't inherit the same vision and faith that was in his parents.

Written into the laws of God are repeated admonitions to teach our children the great truths of the Word of God, His great and mighty acts and deliverance, and to make them understand the righteousness and the judgments of God. There's a reason for that. We were there; they weren't. We've seen it first-hand; they have only heard the tales. Somehow we have to transfer the vision, the faith, and the excitement to our children, because if we don't, who will?

This has been seen throughout the successive church ages all the way back to the beginning. Just 70 to 80 years ago we had wave after wave of excitement pass through our country. Religious fervor was at an all-time high, on-fire revivals were everywhere, souls were coming to the Lord by the thousands, multitudes of sick were supernaturally healed, and the Lord was breathing life into the soul of our nation.

Does anyone remember? Or have we just heard the stories, and are content to sit in our status quo and wait? Does the blame fall on our fathers for not instilling the fear of the Lord in us? Or, like wayward children who would not listen, have we been more enamored with the glitter of this world, the success of life, and the instant gratification of the flesh?

A generation that has not fed off the fire of God will look everywhere else for truth, but will never find it. Eventually, after enough lost generations have wandered far enough and long enough, they will come back to original fountain of life that can be found, not in religion, but only in the breath of the Spirit of God.

I am looking forward to a great revival in this lost generation. They have been starved long enough with a diet of traditional church and a weak gospel without any real power. They are hungry for the fire that comes from off the altar of God.

Once it begins to flow, there will be an army of Christian warriors that will rise up like none that has never been seen … and we will have the greatest revival of all time.

Security

We have been told that Christianity has now spread across the face of the earth, and, although there is severe persecution in many countries, the institution of Christianity in America has reached a level of security and is highly esteemed. After all, statistics show that close to 85% of Americans are Christians of one kind or another. We have arrived. Since we are so secure here, we concentrate on sending our mission trips to places like Mexico, South America, or Africa.

But in prefacing the parable of the rich man and Lazarus, Jesus told us that that which is highly esteemed of men is abomination in the eyes of God.

Have things changed now that we're in a "Christian America?" Can we now rip that admonition out of the Bible? Or do we take a deeper look at our real stand for God? We may walk with a sense of spiritual security, but we need to crucify our own perceptions and see things through God's eyes.

I'm sure the rich man in the parable felt as secure as we do, faring sumptuously in our own church lives. Many flock to "feel good" ministries that preach messages of peace and safety. We have feasted in His presence, done many wonderful works, prophesied in His name, but how will we face the stark realization of eternity at the time of judgment? How have we prepared our lives here? And, more importantly, how have we made provision for the lost?

In Hell, the rich man realized that the things he trusted in could not deliver him. There was no appeal in that courtroom; neither was there any parole—and there was no coming back. It was too late.

In his lifetime, he received good things—a nice peaceful life in church, a sense of spiritual prosperity, no necessity to walk in the fear of God. He had a nice time in his comfort zone. He relied on his pastor and his church life for security. It all sounded so good.

But the words of the wise are as goads and we don't especially like to hear the reproof of the Word of God. They are, however, the way to real life.

The rich man thought if his brethren could just see someone who had risen from the dead that they would come to a realization of the truth, but they had Moses and the prophets. If they wouldn't hearken to the Word of God, they wouldn't believe it if they saw Jesus raised from the dead.

And what did Moses say? Even though he walked in the presence of God, it wasn't enough. He wanted to see God's glory. The routine of church was not enough.

We need desperately to see a manifestation of the glory of God. We need to see a revival fire sweeping our community with power that can be seen and felt. We don't have it, but we can get it. There's only one way. Prayer. Deep, travailing, desperate prayer.

Don't be satisfied with a false sense of security. Reach out for the impossible. God specializes in it. He desperately wants to give to us, but it's up to us to take the Throne of God by storm and claim it in the name of Jesus.

Pray with us that God will move in such a supernatural way that they will hear about it to the ends of the earth, and throughout eternity.

A Little Girl's Prayer

Here's a little prayer that was passed on to me that I thought was pretty timely for us. A twelve-year-old girl in Boston wrote it.

> Now I sit me down in school
> Where praying is against the rule.
> For this great nation under God
> Finds mention of Him very odd.
> If Scripture now the class recites
> It violates the Bill of Rights.
> Anytime my head I bow
> Becomes a federal matter now.
> The law is specific; the law is precise.
> Praying out loud is no longer nice.
> Praying aloud in a public hall
> Upsets those who believe in nothing at all.
> In silence alone we can meditate
> And if God should get the credit-great!
> They are bringing their guns;
> I don't dare bring my Bible,
> To do so, might make me liable.
> So, now Oh Lord, this plea I make;
> Should I be shot in school,
> My soul please take.

How in the world can we not be ashamed? We have not taken the stand for God that we should have all these years. We have allowed our great nation, founded on the Gospel, to slip from our grasp. Why have we allowed things to get so bad that they would invoke a plea such as this from a schoolgirl?

Is it just a simple matter of whether or not we pray out loud at a football game? Or does it strike deeper to the lives we have led as "church" Christians? If our churches had been "on fire" as the Lord has commanded us to be, wouldn't there have been a far greater testimony to the world? What has happened to us? Where are the Billy Sunday's, and the Jonathan Edward's that America has seen in the past that invoked revival in the land and set America ablaze?

We are living in the time that the Lord speaks of as "a great falling away," or, in the Greek, as the great Apostasy. Amos predicted that in the last days there would be a famine in the land for hearing the Word of God.

I am told that the reason our pulpits have smoothed out their messages into a more acceptable social gospel these days is because our preachers believe that the old "hellfire and brimstone" messages only offended people. Even Hollywood has gotten into the act by downplaying on-fire Holy Ghost preachers as being "crazies."

If you will remember back to the Brush Arbor days, however, those messages brought thousands to their knees in repentance and literally changed the fabric of our society. Now, we have preachers that give us messages of "peace and love and prosperity" with no guts and no fire.

The results have been predictable.

Out of the mouth of babes and sucklings hast thou ordained strength because of thine enemies, that thou mightest still the enemy and the avenger.

Psalms 8:2

The Gospel According to René Descartes

Rene Descartes, a philosopher of the Seventeenth Century, wrote the famous phrase, "I think, therefore I am," to expose the nature of our existence in this universe. It's a formidable work and hard for the average person to follow. Nevertheless, it has influenced much of modern thought.

This philosophical rhetoric, if applied to the Gospel, might be re-stated, "I believe, therefore I am saved." But just knowing that God exists does not make you a Christian.

In today's Christian America, we have been exposed to the Gospel from our youth. We have built churches everywhere and have sent missionaries all over the world. Yet all this has accomplished is to make us accountable to what the Lord has asked us to do. We have heard. We know. We understand. But this does not make us righteous before God.

I have heard over and over again, especially here in the Bible Belt, from people who believe in God and therefore assume that they are going to heaven when they die. They subscribe to the Gospel according to Descartes. Is this really what the Bible preaches? Or is there something more to being a Christian than just being what the Epistle of James describes as a "hearer of the Word?"

Human nature seeks equilibrium—a place of security and peace. We strive to find that place where we can rest from our troubles and labor, and finally relax. We would much rather hear a message of peace and prosperity than endure a doctrine that requires us to strive to overcome. It's our nature.

To "relax, and be raptured" sounds so good, but the Bible preaches a message of enduring conflict. It starts in Genesis and ends in Revelation. The Bible says, "there is no discharge from that war." (Ecclesiastes 8:8) War it is, and war it will be until life on this earth is finally all over. We have an adversary, the Devil, and he will not relax until the end. His primary weapon is deception, and he hopes to make us relax, while he works feverishly to deceive us.

But there is a rest available to the people of God, and it is found in the finished work of Christ on the Cross. As Jesus rested from His work, so are we exhorted to walk that same crucified walk as this lowly Nazarene.

If we rest from our own works and the way we would do things, and take upon ourselves to walk in His Spirit, then we allow Him to give us the power to work the works of God.

You will not find true rest anywhere else.

Herod Feared John

Herod feared John, knowing that he was a just man and an holy, and observed him....

Mark 6:20

If you picked up a newspaper today and saw that John the Baptist was holding revival services at a local church, would you drop everything you're doing to make it there? How about Elijah? Or Peter? Would you go because they are famous? Or would you expect to hear a man speak with authority in God?

Souls are drawn to men of God who can stand up in His power and authority. Revivals are poured out on anointed vessels to whom people flock to hear the Word of God, and see the amazing outpouring of the Holy Spirit's work. They came to Jesus to be healed, but stayed to listen because He spoke with authority.

We need that authority today. We are desperate to see a man of God stand up in that kind of power. We have a lot of nice preachers, but we don't have anyone like John the Baptist, Elijah, or Paul. Why is that?

Search the Scriptures and you will find that the kind of power and authority we are referring to only comes only one way—the hard way. We all read and pray, but how many of us STORM the Throne? We all fast, but how many of us crucify our flesh? All this lifts us up to a higher plateau in God, but the real holy boldness, the real strength and power in God, and the genuine authority in God only comes through the fear of the Lord. That is what gives a man strong confidence, makes his face to shine, gives him that entrance into the presence of God's power. Moses' knees smote together, David's flesh trembled, the prophet's spoke of Him being their Dread, Paul feared and trembled. It is the common attribute for every powerful man with authority in God. And we need that today.

In the last twenty to thirty years, the message of the Fear of the Lord has been extracted from our pulpits and has been preached out of our hearts to the point that most Christians don't even believe it anymore. They've been told that "Love" is the most important element. Read carefully, my friend. The Love of God is not possible without the Fear of the Lord. Neither is wisdom, understanding, depth, or power. And we will not see revival or a strong move of God without it.

"Lord, raise us up to have the kind of power and authority in You that John had, that we may see the greatest revival of all time."

God Never Gets Angry

The other day, I was talking to a young woman—and a faithful churchgoer—about the Lord. She explained in gushing terms how she much she believed in the overwhelming love of Jesus.

Now, that's pretty hard to argue with.

For the life of me, I have never been able to understand why God, in all His majesty, was willing to come down to this earth and transform Himself into human flesh, just a piece of dirt, for us.

You know, it's not like we've been good boys and girls, and we deserve it. After all, it got so bad once, that He destroyed every living, breathing thing except for a small handful. You would have thought that the lesson had been learned, but, within a few generations, mankind was back at it again, and this time with a vengeance. Human flesh just loves to wallow in sin.

So God sent messenger after messenger—powerful men of God that had an incredible witness in word, in signs, and in wonders, but people still didn't get it. The prophets were killed to get them out of the way, and people wondered why they were under the curses of God.

God finally sends His only begotten Son. Jesus has the most powerful testimony of all. I dare say that everybody knew who He was. Some hung onto every word as if their life depended on it. Others tried to make excuses and find some way around the righteousness of God. Still others hated Him so much, the only way they could shut Him up was to kill Him, and they picked a slow torture to do it. That's how much the flesh, when it gives itself over to sin and pride, hates God.

But get this! He knew all along that He would go to the Cross. Amazing! What's more, that was the original plan from way back in the Garden of Eden!

I don't get it. How could God care that much for a bunch of rebellious mud pies that will not do what they were supposed to? When we make something that doesn't work, don't we just throw it in the trash and start over?

But, I do know this—there are those who love God and His righteousness so much, that they would do anything to serve him. Anything. I guess those are the ones that Heaven is reserved for.

And the others? Back to Plan A for them. (Or is that Plan H?)

OK. So God loves us more than we can ever know. I understand. But then this young woman rambles on about how Jesus and God never get angry. He always did everything with so much love and gentleness.

About now, I'm scratching my head wondering what Bible she's reading. Is this the Disney version? I know we've got some real smooth versions out there that water down a lot of stuff, but really, "God never gets angry?" The original King James says that He is angry with the wicked everyday! After all, Jesus whipped them out of the Temple!

When we rely on our own perceptions to define how we want the personality of God to be, we will end up running completely contrary to the simple precepts found in His Word. Our desire to create a God in our own image comes from our unwillingness to give up the desires of the flesh. If we can just design a Gospel that will, in some way, excuse sin, then we can escape having to repent. The lie that has worked ever since Satan tried it on Eve is that God loves us so much that we shall not surely die.

Cool idea! Now, if we can design a religion around that idea, we can out-maneuver the call to holiness, without which (my Bible says) no man shall see the Lord. How about, if all we have to do is count a few beads, light some candles, and mutter some repetitious prayers. Or better yet, we can tell people that all they have to do is say a prayer one time in their lives and they will never have to worry about it again.

You say no one will believe it, but I'm telling you it will work! It worked for Eve, and it will work for all those who would rather believe in a God that thinks like we do, instead of liking what He says.

God loves us so much that He never gets angry.

Boy, that sure sounds good. What a great religion to live by. But I sure wouldn't want to die by it.

Excuses

There's an old saying that an excuse is just an excuse is just an excuse. It's amazing how many excuses we can come up with to justify doing the things we want to do and to slide around the things we don't want to do.

When we look over all the different religions available, and the various doctrines within each one, we can't help wondering which is the right way. So we pick one that suits us the best, and we pursue that direction. Who can convince us that we're wrong? After all, isn't one religion as good as another? Aren't we supposed to be tolerant of one another?

That kind of thinking can ultimately get us into a lot of trouble.

Being comfortable doesn't necessarily mean being right, but it sure is the path of least resistance. The problem is that we will all stand in judgment before the same God, with whom there is only one way and one Truth. The trick is to seek the one way that He dictates, and not allow ourselves to be persuaded to follow a path that is more in tune with the way we would like, just because it sounds good.

We're told that strict adherence to His Word will tell us the right way to live, but how many of us will quote some well-worn phrases that we've heard from some other person to justify what we want to hear? The Bible says that the Spirit of God bears witness to the truth. Does that mean that every time we feel good at church, we're OK, and we can do whatever we want to? Is that all it takes to be right with God? Can we use that as an excuse at the judgment bar? Doesn't it take a little more than just being satisfied with the appearance of a form of godliness?

Proverbs says that they who seek the Lord understand all things (Proverbs 28:5). Perhaps there needs to be a desire to seek a little deeper than surface "religiousness" to really discover the ways of God. Perhaps it's all a test to see if we really have a heart that cries out to God for more than "church as usual." Maybe we need to seek Him with our whole heart. As it is written, "It is the glory of God to conceal a thing, the honor of kings is to search out a matter" (Proverbs 25:2).

Hmmmm. That puts a little different perspective on it, doesn't it?

Here's the kicker. The Word of God refers to a time soon coming when there will be a one-world religion. There is an hour of temptation coming that will try the whole world. Will we go along with the flow because it is easier and much more tolerant? Or will we settle it in our hearts to find that one true way to God and make our stand with the righteous, no matter what the cost?

> *Enter ye in at the strait gate: for wide is the gate, and broad is the way, that leadeth to destruction, and many there be which go in thereat: Because strait is the gate, and narrow is the way, which leadeth unto life, and few there be that find it.*
>
> *Matthew 7:13,14*

Love Offerings

The old King James translators correctly used the word "charity" in 1 Corinthians 13.

Today, where we are inundated with "relationships," the word "love" has taken on the meaning of a warm and fuzzy emotion to us, but God defines it as the keeping of His commandments.

There's a bit of a difference there. Charity goes beyond an ethereal feeling or emotion, because charity is the giving of oneself *out* of love to see souls get saved. And stay saved. Charity is love in action.

In broadcast after broadcast, we see one evangelist after another end their programs with their hands out for a "love offering." Oh, they wring their hands and talk of all the wonderful things their ministry is doing, and of all the wonderful tapes and books they have made available for us—if only we will send them a "love offering" of $24.95.

I have a few problems with this routine. I never read where Jesus had such sophisticated and complicated philosophies as they do. He spoke to the people on their own terms. But I guess if you want to sell something, it's got to be something new. Everybody's already heard the old stuff in the Bible.

When Jesus broke the bread and fishes, however, he commanded His disciples to *give* it to the multitude. We're supposed to feed the sheep, not fleece them.

Second, they always say the same three things: 1) their video is soooo powerful, and 2) it'll change your life. (Geez! And here I thought it was the Word of God that was so powerful and could change people's lives.) And 3) they really want you to have this thing.

I know how much money it takes to put the Gospel out, but since when is God broke? Did He lose all His money in the stock market or something? Besides, tithes and offerings are supposed to be determined out of your heart before God. Where did they get the authority to dictate the terms and amounts of your offering?

There's a popular saying that states, "What would Jesus do?" I'll tell you what He did when he was here in the flesh. He whipped the moneychangers out of the Temple for selling merchandise in the House of God. If they've got such a powerful message that will change your life, then why don't they give it away free? That's what Jesus did.

Friend, don't be fooled by men who make a career out of the Gospel in this way. Charity is the essence of real Christianity. Let's get back to the great things in the Word of God; stick with the basics, and look to the Lord to lead us and guide us in the way. Give your tithe to a soul-winning work, where the preacher is not afraid to stand up for righteousness, to keep us in the reproof of God's Word wherein is the way of life, and bring down Holy Ghost conviction to keep us out of Hell. Those are the works of charity, and that is where you will find the seeds of revival.

God will take care of the rest.

Blind as Balaam

And Balaam rose up in the morning, and saddled his ass, and went with the princes of Moab.
Numbers 22:21

Here was a man called out of Mesopotamia, who was recognized as a supposed prophet of God, and offered riches and glory to do the bidding of a worldly king.

Not satisfied with his first message from God, Balaam was more than ready to rush off in the morning after his 2nd request to follow the princes of Moab. He didn't wait for them to come to him as God had commanded, but made the presumption that God had changed His mind and he was heading off towards great honor.

Why is it that he could not see the Angel standing in the way? Was it because his eyes were blinded and he could not see? God had to speak through a jackass (not exactly one of the noblest of beasts) to reprove him one last time, as He often does to us today. But when he started walking in the fear of God, he had no choice but to fulfill God's mission, and lost his dream of worldly riches in the process.

Why was he later, then, slain by the Israelites? Was it because he had made this mistake? Or was it because, after he left to go back to his people in Mesopotamia, he realized what the key was to nullifying the blessings he had just spoken on Israel. He knew that if he taught Moab to befriend Israel and cause them to sin, that God would have to curse them. He must have turned around and come back to do this, because he was slain in Moab, not Mesopotamia. He just never did get the message, did he?

Today, we see huge TV ministries claiming all kinds of wonderful things happening with them worldwide and ending up each broadcast with a convincing plea for more money. If we will just give our money to them, they claim that all sorts of wonderful things will happen in our lives. Although they claim all sorts of wonderful things happening in their ministries, yet we see throughout the Scriptures, in Joel, Amos, the Prophets, 2 Thessalonians, Matthew. 24, Revelation, that before we see this last great revival of the church, there will be widespread apostasy, famine, and spiritual desolation.

Whom do we believe?

Make no mistake. There is coming an outpouring of the Lord's Spirit like never before. It is coming, and it will rattle our teeth when it comes. But beforehand, the Body of Christ will have to come to a place of repentance and cry out to the Living God to cleanse us and forgive us. We do not have this great revival yet, and sending money off to these golden edifices will not get us off the hook or buy us a place in God.

God wants our hearts first.

We must first come to a place where we realize that we are not where we should be in our walk with God. And we have to want to get to that place more than life itself. Then we can repent and cry out to God for revival.

We've got a ways to go. Be careful that you do not make the mistake of taking a shortcut that will lead you down the wrong path.

I asked the Lord why these ministers cannot see this clearly? The answer was simple.

They're as blind as Balaam was, and for the same reasons.

Human Nature

I remember, as a kid in college back in the 60s, listening to a rally by the young revolutionaries of the day that were all fired up against the government. At the time, it was the "in thing" to support a revolution. One rabble-rouser after another would get up behind the microphone and scream and yell louder than the last guy. I never heard a clear message, just a bunch of emotionally charged posturing that was designed to whip the crowd into a frenzy.

Finally, some kid got up and delivered what I thought to be a clear thoughtful defense for the opposition. Reason did not win out that day. The boo's and threats leveled at him were frightening. Emotion rather than careful thought too often rules human nature. We hear what we want to hear, and we tend to believe what we want to believe.

The other extreme is not much better. When we analyze things down to the molecular level, we lose sight of the big picture. Our focus becomes pinpointed on meaningless details rather than the original purpose.

So it is with Christianity. It's like being in a sailboat at sea. It is the wind of God's Spirit that will drive you to where He wants you to go, but by gosh, you can't just sit there and expect the boat to go by itself. You do have to raise the sail! On the other hand, if you try to break out the oars to do it by works, you won't get very far.

When we are comfortable with something, we find it so easy to slide into an easy acceptance, and there is little reason to pursue it any further. This makes for a real nice "church on Sunday" mentality. We tend to resist anything that would suggest change, especially if it rocks the comfortable boat that we are drifting in.

Then there are the scholars that pursue theological scholasticism to the point that the very essence of Christianity is overlooked. They clamber up the Tree of the Knowledge of Good and Evil looking for fruit that will make them wise, and they ignore the warning that "knowledge puffeth up and charity edifieth. (1 Corinthians 8:1)" There won't be an exam at the Judgment Bar of God on what you know—just on what you have done.

I see in the Scriptures that Jesus Christ made a strong stand against both of these mentalities. He left us a pretty clear testimony for us to follow—and they crucified Him for it.

Let us be careful not to seek after philosophy, or religion, or books, or how we want things to be, but to seek the face of God to walk in His Spirit and to follow Him. He is the Door, and His Word is a lamp unto our feet.

There is no other way.

Modern Day Prophets

And it shall come to pass in that day, that the prophets shall be ashamed every one of his vision, when he hath prophesied; neither shall they wear a rough garment to deceive:

Zechariah 13:4

It seems that we are always hearing about some new "prophetic ministry" that has risen up. Our first reaction is to be excited to hear some new word from God. So many times, however, we hear the same message that we've already heard from the last "prophetic ministry." The themes usually center on the wonderful promises of all the good things that God is going to do for us shortly, and we leave feeling really good about ourselves. Often, these people with this "gift of prophecy" will tell us something personal that will soon happen in our personal lives. We're getting a new car, or we will soon take a trip, or there will be a change in our lives.

How wonderful it is to hear a personal message straight to us from God Himself. It's almost like having your own personal Christian horoscope.

Rarely do we hear prophetic messages of doom and gloom, judgment, repentance, and the Fear of the Lord. Those kinds of messages don't draw crowds and they don't sell tickets. We don't want to hear bad stuff; we want to hear good stuff. We don't want to hear something that will make us afraid; we want to hear something that makes us feel good. As we see crowds flocking to "feel good" ministries, we see more and more of these "prophetic" ministries pop up.

Is that what prophets of God are supposed to be like? Are today's prophets little more than fortune-tellers and Gypsies? How do they and their messages measure up against the prophets in the Bible and the messages that they brought forth?

Everybody wants to be an Elijah, but nobody wants to pay the price. I don't see any of the prophets in the Bible jumping up and down for joy over the calling that was placed upon them. The job of prophet is hard, and the price that is required is more than the human flesh is willing to pay.

Foretelling the future is not the job of a prophet; it is a consequence of the job. Ezekiel tells us that the real job of a prophet is to stand in the gaps of the walls that are broken down, and call the people of God back to repentance (Ezekiel 13:5). Micah says that it is to declare unto them their sin and transgression (Micah 3:8). They don't speak messages to make us feel comfortable; what they have to say makes us feel uncomfortable. It is a small wonder that real prophets are always despised.

Only in times of severe persecution and affliction, does God send messages of peace and conciliation to encourage and strengthen His people to hold on to His promises. In times of prosperity and relative peace, however, the message is about repentance and soon coming judgments. Most of what we hear today, however, are messages of prosperity, peace, love, and beautiful things. There are severe sentences of judgment written in the Bible for false prophets that prophesy of peace when the Lord has not spoken through them.

As it says in Proverbs 9:8, a wise man loves reproof. I'd rather have God drag me off to the ol' woodshed any day and scare the Devil out of me, than be appeased by Gypsies that weaken my resolve to seek the face of God in fear and trembling.

The Spirit of Whoredom

I have said that the Lord wants to move in our communities in a great and mighty way—in supernatural ways that it will be spoken of for years to come. What a wonderful opportunity we have before us to open the door for this to happen!

But there are always conditions with God. Revival fire does not just fall out of the sky. There is a formula that is required. You can read it in the Book of Joel, in Daniel, in Nehemiah, Chronicles, and Revelation. The people of God must come to a place of realization that they can no longer be settled on their lees, as it says in Zephaniah 1:12, a place where we are at ease. We need to be in a place of repentance and start crying out with all our hearts for God to move.

Instead of hearing messages of Holy Ghost conviction that bring us to a place of repentance before God, however, all we ever hear—especially on TV and radio—are messages of peace and love.

But what kinds of messages did the prophets in the Word of God preach? From the first prophet in the Old Testament to John the Revelator in the New Testament, the message is to repent and walk in the fear of God. The job of a prophet is to declare to the people of God their sin, not to give messages of peace and prosperity, or to beg for money so you can buy your way into blessings.

There is a spirit of whoredom with the world that Hosea warns about which will enter the church and bring it into a false sense of prosperity and security, and so reject the cries of the prophets. Jeremiah cried out to his people to repent, but they turned their ears away and ended up being carried off to Babylon. We also, if we do not hearken, will end up being carried away to the modern-day Babylon, the one-world church.

It is time to gather together a solemn assembly and rend our hearts, not our garments, and cry out to God for revival. There's a price to be paid. If we will not pay it, we will shortly reach that time when the Lord says, "That's enough," and He will turn from us and look for someone else. We could end up in that rut of "church as usual" that we like so much, thinking that everything is beautiful, until that great day of judgment descends upon us. Then the covering will be ripped off our eyes and we will see how we had been seduced into an easy Gospel and left without oil in our lamps.

Let us find a way to gather together in prayer to receive the revival that the Lord wants so desperately to give us. Lost souls out there depend upon us to pray for this great and mighty move of God.

Focus on Others

And he could there do no mighty work, save that he laid his hands upon a few sick folk, and healed them.

Mark 6:5

All Jesus could do was heal a few sick folk? Boy, that would have been enough to get *me* all excited.

But the people in that town just didn't get it. And Jesus marveled because of their unbelief. What was the matter with these people? What more did they want? There was an underlying problem here with these people that kept them from experiencing a great move of God. But then again, haven't we seen the same today?

Do you believe in God's supernatural power to heal? Do you *really* believe? What's more, do you care? I have prayed for people who have been supernaturally healed while being prayed for, yet found that it generated very little excitement in the Christians that knew about it. Why is that?

There was the girl who had been diagnosed with sixty distinct demonic personalities who had come crying for help, and the Lord delivered her with a gigantic "whoosh." There was the little girl who had AIDS with little time to live, but the Lord healed her instantly when I prayed for her. Then there was the man who had leukemia so bad that his head was swollen like a basketball. He could take you to the very spot where he was standing when we prayed and the Lord crashed down on him and completely healed him. And there are many more. This is pretty supernatural stuff! And it happens today just like it did in Jesus' time. But what's the reaction of Christians and of ministers who hear about things like this? "Oh, that's nice." Ho hum.

That's nice? You know what—I marvel!

I suppose that, since it didn't happen to these particular ministers personally, it just didn't have quite the same effect on them as it did on me. Human nature makes us generally more concerned with ourselves than with others. It's a fact of life. And it shows itself in the type of Gospel that we hear preached over our pulpits today, and the effects it has on our lives.

We flock by the thousands to ministries that preach a "feel good" message and tell us "smooth" things. Prosperity ministries abound and make no pretense about what their focus is on. We love to hear that God loves us, and that we can rest in a permissive gospel.

When we gather up at the front of the altar on Sunday, what is it that everyone prays for? Ourselves—our own problems; our own needs and desires. Some altar call. Every once in a while, someone will throw out a bone for lost souls, but it's usually a real quickie so we can get back to praying for ourselves.

Think I'm being cynical? Take a circuit tour of your churches and see if I'm not telling the truth.

Real revival never comes to those who are satisfied or concerned with their own well-being. It only comes to those who, in desperate prayer and crying out to God from the depths of their hearts for others, want more than a dead church service and are willing to pay whatever price to see souls come to salvation and escape the horrors of Hell for eternity.

There are many such people out there who are desperate for a move of God. Don't be discouraged. Keep storming the Throne of God, and get excited, 'cause we ain't seen nothin' yet.

The Church as a Bride

In like manner also, that women adorn themselves in modest apparel, with shamefacedness and sobriety; not with broided hair, or gold, or pearls, or costly array; But (which becometh women professing godliness) with good works.

1 Timothy 2:9,10

In the above passage, I don't think Paul was trying to tell women how to dress. I realize he wasn't married and didn't know what it was like to live with a woman, but he couldn't be that dumb. I don't think that how you wear your hair, makeup, or earrings are issues of eternal significance. I believe that Paul was addressing the Bride of Christ, the church—that same virtuous woman that we find in Proverbs 31.

Throughout the Bible we see a reference to the true church as the bride and false churches as harlots. God, from the very beginning, has established the marriage relationship between a man and his wife as the foundational analogy of Christ and His Church. Everything about marriage, from the courtship to the kids, is significant. Adultery, polygamy, modesty, and maternity are all very significant analogies of our marriage to Jesus Christ. The marriage contract is, in essence, a holy vow to serve the Lord.

Notwithstanding she shall be saved in childbearing....

(1 Timothy 2:15)

Does this mean that all women are cursed because of Eve and are destined for Hell if they don't have babies? Does that make any sense at all? Or has it occurred to you that a church that does not win souls is like a wife that is barren, an unfruitful branch on the vine. The very first commandment that God gave was on the fifth day of creation—be fruitful and multiply—and that embodies the very essence of Christianity, which is charity.

I don't want to belong to a very nice church that is not winning any souls. Nice place, but only maintaining its status quo. There is something missing in that church's marriage relationship with Christ. A lukewarm church is a bride who is in love with someone else other than the Lord Jesus Christ. He is looking for a bride who is passionately in love with Him, and, like Rachel in Genesis 30:1, is desperate to bring forth fruit for her husband.

The Marriage Supper of the Lamb is about to be served. The invitations have been sent, the guests are assembling, and the bride has made herself ready.

> *And the Spirit and the bride say, Come. And let him that heareth say, Come. And let him that is athirst come....*
>
> *(Revelations 22:17)*

The Wedding Feast

The kingdom of heaven is like unto a certain king, which made a marriage for his son....
Matthew 22:2

What happens when you throw a dinner party and nobody comes? Can you imagine being in a situation like that, looking at all the food, the salads, the party decorations, the beautifully set long white dinner table, the balloons...and nobody's shows up. Kind of an ugly feeling, isn't it?

What happened? You sent out the invitations, didn't you? Everyone knew. They were supposed to be your friends. What was the problem? Why didn't they want to come? It was to be such a grand party! You had made wonderful preparations, ordered the very best of food and drink, and engaged the finest of orchestras. What was it they didn't like?

Maybe it wasn't the party as much as the personality. Maybe it wasn't the food or the music or the setting. Maybe it was you. So you send others to out to find out what happened and they bring you back a bunch of excuses a mile long. All good reasons, but the fact remains that they just didn't show.

And the Lord says that this is like the kingdom of heaven? Makes you think, doesn't it? Jesus said you that are his friends *if* you do whatsoever he commands you.

I believe that the invitations have been sent and the call has been issued to us to pray and fast for an outpouring of the Spirit of the Lord to bring about a great revival in our communities. How many of us have answered that call? Instead, how many of us have felt that by going to church on Sunday, we are able to slide around the calling that has been made on our lives?

We call ourselves friends, but have we been too busy making excuses to stand up and take on the challenges that the Lord has given us? Was the invitation sent to gather ourselves in a church so we can listen to a "feel good" message about ourselves, or has the call been made to seek the face of God with fasting and prayer for an old-fashioned, heaven-sent, Holy Ghost revival for the lost?

I have said this over the air, and will say it in print: The Lord will give the churches a certain space of time to repent—and they won't repent. Then He will raise up stones in their place. That's exactly how it will happen. This isn't a pleasant message to receive; and neither is it a pleasant message to give. But it is the message of the Lord.

So what happens next?

> *Then the master of the house being angry said to his servant, Go out quickly into the streets and lanes of the city, and bring in hither the poor, and the maimed, and the halt, and the blind.*
>
> *(Luke 14:21)*

> *...and the wedding was furnished with guests.*
>
> *(Matthew 22:10)*

Go, and do thou likewise.

Conclusion

I HAVE DELIVERED TO YOU THAT WHICH HAS BEEN DELIVERED TO ME. CERTAINLY, this is not a finished book, any more than the book of Acts, which has no Amen. This is part of a tapestry that only you can continue to weave in your own life.

If these chapters have been nothing more than interesting reading for you, then I have failed in my mission. Hopefully, however, they have pricked you, convicted you, encouraged you, maybe even made you mad, but at least, inspired you on to something greater in God.

It's your turn now. They say that in a few years there will be as many people alive on the face of the earth as have ever lived throughout all time. What an opportunity! One-half of humanity lies at our doorstep. Will you do whatever the Lord asks of you? Will you take the answers to life to a world that is dying?

Before you jump to an impulsive "Yes" there are two things you need. One is faith in the Gospel as the only truth upon the face of the earth, and the other is an inspiration to drive you to a place of power in God. If you are not empowered by the Spirit of God, you will not accomplish anything lasting. There has to be a fire burning in your heart before you can ever hope to spread the flame. If you don't have either of these, go before Him and ask for both. I guarantee He will answer your prayer.

I pray that this book has been both an inspiration and a challenge. In the ages to come when tales are retold and the victories recounted, let it be said that a fire was ignited in our souls that burned to the ends of the earth.

Go forth and light the fire of revival in preparation for our soon-coming King.

Dalen Garris is a minister of the Gospel based in Waxahachie, Texas and has been in the ministry in one form or another since 1970. All correspondence can be addressed to him at the address below.

Fire in the Hole is a broadcast outreach of Horizon Ministries. Our radio broadcast is heard weekly in several foreign countries, including Israel. It is also broadcast across the United States on the satellite radio station Sky Angel.

The audio broadcasts are also posted on our website, www.RevivalFire.org and can be downloaded for free in MP3 format. Cassette tapes of the messages can be mailed to you by subscription.

The weekly column, *Fire in the Hole*, is printed in several newspapers in the U.S. and emailed around the world. They are also posted on the website. If you would like to have the column emailed to you free of charge, sign up on our free Mail List on the website or by correspondence.

If you would like Dalen Garris to speak at your church or organization, contact us at the phone number below for times and schedules.

Dalen Garris, Horizon Ministries
P.O. Box 822
Waxahachie, TX 75168
USA
(972) 938-8502

Printed in the United States
92321LV00006B/1-36/A

9 781414 103761